Nobody is more the master of the clear intriguing sentence than Fisher Humphreys. He beckons us toward those important and difficult ideas of Scripture we need to grasp, and soon we find ourselves engaged in effortless, enjoyable learning. Children understand him. Scholars are afraid to miss his work, for he makes the obscure clear and the tedious delightful. Read and find a new addiction to the wisdom of Fisher Humphreys.

—Dr. Calvin Miller,
professor, Beeson Divinity School,
and author of *The Singer Trilogy* and *Loving God Up Close*

Fisher Humphreys is one of the best followers of Christ that I know; he is also one of the most intelligent. He has the gift of communicating with different audiences in their language. His major concern, however, is using his gifts and his background to understand what it means to be a Christian and to communicate that understanding to others in the community of faith in language that they can understand. This new book is a good product of that purpose. He has sifted the New Testament to identify the various images that are used to describe believers, e.g., disciple, steward, friend, etc. He has interpreted those images to help us understand what it means to be a follower of Jesus. This book is his contribution to help people who genuinely wish to live out the Christian life to achieve their goal.

—Dr. Malcolm Tolbert,
former professor, New Orleans Baptist Theological Seminary
and Southeastern Baptist Theological Seminary

Dr. Fisher Humphreys's book I Have Called You Friends *challenged me to rethink who I am in Jesus Christ. I earned a sincere appreciation of what it means to be an apprentice and friend of Christ. It stopped me and made me reexamine the stewardship of my spiritual gifts and personal resources. It convinced me of my place in Christ as a soldier, a slave, and an athlete. It caused me to rethink my place in Christ's church.* I Have Called You Friends *showed me the importance of prayer and meditation and forgiveness, and called me to refocus on what it means to be Christ's disciple. Through Dr. Humphreys's biblical wisdom, simple style, and clear communication, I suspect his readers will experience a certain spiritual transformation and renewal.*

—Denise George,
author of *God's Heart, God's Hands* and *Come to the Quiet*

When we became Christ followers, we cast off the role of sinner and took on new dimensions of the abundant life in Him. Throughout His life on earth Jesus clarified that role through the use of images—disciple, soldier, athlete, and others. Fisher Humphreys, in his book I Have Called You Friends, *highlights and clarifies those images and challenges us to make them more fully our own. This book should be required reading for all Christ's friends!*

—Dr. Dellanna O'Brien,
former executive director, national WMU

Here is a book to instruct your mind and heart. Entering into its pages is like entering once again into the classroom of this favorite and noted professor of theology as Scripture comes alive through the New Testament images of the Christ follower. It is profoundly simple and simply profound.

—Dr. Carol McCall Richardson,
former president, Tennessee WMU

I Have Called You Friends

I Have Called You Friends

New Testament Images
That Challenge Us to Live as
CHRIST FOLLOWERS

FISHER HUMPHREYS

new
hope
PUBLISHERS

Birmingham, Alabama

New Hope® Publishers
P. O. Box 12065
Birmingham, AL 35202-2065
www.newhopepublishers.com

Library of Congress Cataloging-in-Publication Data
Humphreys, Fisher.
I have called you friends : New Testament images that challenge us to live as Christ followers / Fisher Humphreys.
p. cm.
ISBN 1-56309-945-4 (soft cover)
1.   Christian life-Biblical teaching. 2. Bible. N.T.-Criticism, interpretation, etc. I. Title.
BS2545.C48H86 2005
248.4—dc22
2004031099

ISBN: 1-56309-945-4
N054118 • 0505 • 7.5M1

Dedication

To
Camille Grace Humphreys
and
Kate Elizabeth Humphreys,
Our Beloved Granddaughters

Table of Contents

BY TIMOTHY GEORGE

T*heologia est scientia vivendo deo,* "Theology is the knowledge of how to live in the presence of God." This is the best definition of theology I have ever found. It comes from a book, *The Marrow of Sacred Divinity*, written by the famous Puritan theologian William Ames, which was first published in 1623. Ames's volume was the first theology textbook used at Harvard College and it remained a popular source of devotional reading and Christian reflection for many years.

Why do I like Ames' definition of theology so much? Because it brings together two elements often held at arm's length in the history of the church: the idea that theology is an orderly body of knowledge—a "science," to use the Latin root—and the fact that this body of knowledge has a divinely intended purpose, namely, to enable us to live every moment of our lives with joy and intentionality, in the presence of the true and living God. To focus on one without the other is to be a half-Christian. Theology divorced from life is arid intellectualism. A Christian life not based on sound biblical principles will end up in sterile activism or sentimental fluff. As usual, Jesus said it best: "You shall love the Lord your God with all your heart, and with all your soul, and with all your mind, and with all your strength" (Mark 12:30).

This book brings together head and heart, theology

and life, in a way that makes sense of what it means to follow Jesus Christ in today's world. Taking his cue from Paul Minear's classic study of images of the church in the New Testament, Fisher Humphreys has chosen ten major images used by the Bible to describe the earliest followers of Jesus. Why images? Because images help us to visualize as well as conceptualize. Theology that is true to the Bible contains both a propositional and an incarnational dimension. The Bible tells us that some things are true, and that other things are false. It is filled with ideas and concepts, with principles and doctrines, about God, human beings, the world, salvation, angels, demons, heaven, hell. Part of the theologian's job is to study these ideas and to try to make sense of them in light of the Bible's overarching storyline of creation and redemption. But in fact, we frequently first encounter the reality to which these biblical ideas point through images.

This is most evident, I think, in some of the spirituals drawn from the African-American tradition. For example, "Sometimes I Feel Like a Motherless Child" tells us something of the sense of abandonment and grief felt by an orphaned child, a poignant expression of living in a broken, sinful world. Likewise, "He's a Battle-Axe" recalls God's sovereign triumph over the forces of evil. The beautiful lyric, "There Is a Balm in Gilead," draws on a biblical image to describe redemption and hope. Good theology will neglect neither the propositional nor the incarnational aspect of biblical revelation, for throughout Scripture God shows

14

His true identity in both word and deed, in acts of self-disclosure and in stories and images that help us to enter into their meaning.

The ten images Dr. Humphreys has chosen to highlight in this book—disciple, servant, steward, soldier, athlete, traveler, priest, child, friend, and guest—are all drawn from the New Testament, most of them from the life and ministry of Jesus Himself. I like the Christocentric focus of this book. In some churches, when a Scripture passage from one of the Gospels is read, the congregation stands in honor of those inspired accounts of Jesus' person and work. This does not mean, of course, that Matthew, say, is more inspired than 2 Thessalonians, but it is a way of emphasizing the centrality of Jesus Christ and His incarnation—the Word was made flesh (John 1:14)—in salvation history, in the Bible itself, and in the lives of all who still seek to follow Jesus. These images take us back to those unforgettable events and the power they still have for all who call Jesus Lord: a poor beggar unexpectedly invited to a lavish banquet; a child on the margins of a crowd singled out as the object lesson of love; tax collectors, strangers, women of the gutters made intimates of the Messiah; the friend of sinners calling sinners to be His friends.

Of all the chapters in this book the one I like best is the one on friendship. Of all the titles Jesus gave to His disciples, none is more awesome than "friend." This term is all the more remarkable when we consider that, as Paul puts it, we were all once God's "enemies" (Romans 5:10). Through the life, death, and resurrection of Jesus Christ, we who were once "far off"—estranged, alienated, indifferent, and even hostile to the heart of the Father's love—have been brought by God's grace within the intimate circle of the Savior's friends.

There is another reason why I like the chapter on friendship so much. Fisher Humphreys is my friend and I see in him so many Christ-like traits of one who is truly a friend of Jesus. I have been drawn closer to Christ through my friendship with Fisher and I commend him to you as a worthy guide in the pilgrimage of faith.

—*Timothy George*
  Epiphany 2005

TIMOTHY GEORGE is dean of Beeson Divinity School of Samford University and an executive editor of *Christianity Today*.

About fifty years ago an American New Testament scholar was asked to prepare a study of the images of the church in the New Testament, and he found 96 of them. The scholar's name is Paul S. Minear, and he is now an emeritus professor of Yale Divinity School. His study was first published in 1960 with the title *Images of the Church in the New Testament.* I read it sometime in the 1970s, and it gave me the idea for this present book.

In the initial chapter of his book, Dr. Minear observed that in our modern, scientific world, we tend to assume that we understand a thing best when we are able to measure it and to grasp it rationally. We also tend to assume that when we use images to speak about something, we do so not as a means of understanding it for ourselves but only as a means of communicating with others. Minear then observed that the reverse was true in the world of the New Testament; images were thought to be the best way to understand things, especially things that are mysterious.[1]

This seems to me to be true, and important. I invite the readers of this book, which is a study of some of the images used of Christ followers in the New Testament, to join me in adopting the attitude of the New Testament era. I hope that you will read this book not merely as a way of learning how to communicate better to others the meaning of being a Christ follower, but as a way of understanding that meaning for yourself.

Images are products of the imagination, and we understand them and our lives best when we use our own imaginations. Margaret Miles said, "In order to live a Christian life, one must first imagine such a life, must visualize what it might look like and feel like."[2] In this book, I will try to distinguish between the meanings of the images that are spelled out in the New Testament, and meanings that may present themselves to our imaginations today but which were not spelled out by the writers of the New Testament.

In the years since I first read Dr. Minear's book, I have spoken dozens of times and in a variety of venues about images of Christ followers in the New Testament. I talked about the images in some of my classes at New Orleans Baptist Theological Seminary and in some of my classes at Beeson Divinity School. Occasionally I led church retreats in which we had the opportunity to discuss for several hours the relevance of the images for churches and for individual Christ followers today. I also have preached sermons about several of the images.

Unfortunately, I did not keep a record of all these events. I remember some of them vividly, but I feel sure I have forgotten others, especially those that took place twenty or more years ago. For that reason I have decided not to mention any names here; I do not want to risk omitting the names of people who have conversed with me about these things.

Nevertheless, I want to register here my appreciation to the church groups and students and other persons who across these twenty-five or so years have helped me to understand better these biblical images and their relevance to our lives today. I thank you for your insights, about which I often made notes, and I hope that what I have written here has done justice to your contributions.

This is a book of Bible study, and in the course of it I have referred to and quoted hundreds of passages of Scripture. In each case I have attempted to employ a translation that seems to me to communicate as clearly as possible the truth being discussed. In order to do this, I have made use of five different translations.

Readers who are puzzled about the use of so many translations might consider a simple question: How should you translate the Spanish phrase, *Buenos días?* A literal translation is *Good day.* However, *Buenos días* is a standard greeting in Spanish, and *Good day* is not a standard greeting in the United States today (apparently it is in Australia). So *Buenos días* might be better translated with a standard greeting such as *Hello, Hi, Good morning, Good afternoon,* or even *Nice to see you.* We need different translations of the Bible for the same reason we need different translations of *Buenos días.*

The translation I have used most often in this book is the *New Revised Standard Version,* so when I quote it, I do not indicate the translation.

In several places, especially when I am quoting from Proverbs, I used the *Today's English Version* published by the American Bible Society; I identified those references as TEV.

In a few passages I quoted the King James Version of the Bible, and I indicated that by KJV.

And on rare occasions I quoted the New English Bible (indicated by NEB) and its revised edition, the Revised English Bible (REB).

My wife Caroline and I have two grandchildren. Observing them has helped me learn afresh some of the insights that appear in chapter eight. I have dedicated this book to these two beautiful sisters, Camille and Kate, with love.

This book is a study of New Testament teachings about Christian living, and I have written it for Christians who are interested in understanding themselves and the life God is calling them to live. Christians are people who have heard the story of Jesus Christ and who have responded by trusting in Him as their savior and Lord. All Christians are called to be followers of Christ.

In the New Testament the call to follow Christ is sounded repeatedly, and it takes several quite different formats. I will give three examples.

RULES

The most natural form of the biblical call to Christian living is as a list of rules; sometimes the rules are expressed as commands, sometimes as principles.

Some Christians think that although the Old Testament contains rules such as the Ten Commandments, the New Testament contains no rules. However, that is not the case. The New Testament contains rules just as the Old Testament does. There is an example in Romans 12:9–13:

Hate what is evil, hold fast to what is good; love one another with mutual affection; outdo one another in showing honor. Do not lag in zeal, be ardent in spirit, serve the Lord. Rejoice in hope, be patient in suffering, persevere in prayer. Contribute to the needs of the saints; extend hospitality to strangers.

Those are a dozen rules, listed one after another. In the remainder of Romans 12 and in the following chapters, Paul recorded several dozen additional rules by which Christians should live. Clearly the New Testament contains rules for Christian living.

Some Christians dislike the fact that they are called to live by rules. As often as not, their resistance to rules is a product of experiences they have had. Perhaps their parents were legalistic and unloving people, or perhaps they had a schoolteacher who was harsh and demanding about keeping trivial rules. In any case, they experience rules as oppressive, and they cannot imagine a life of rules that is not legalistic, self-righteous, and hypocritical. They gravitate to the idea that Christ has set them free from rules. They know they are called to live as Christians, but they find it difficult to hear that call when it takes the form of rules.

This is understandable. Fortunately, there are other forms of that call to Christian living that may be helpful to them.

WISDOM

In the Old Testament era many faithful Jews developed an appreciation for wisdom. A person who is wise is a person who knows how life is supposed to be lived; wisdom is a mastery of life and its challenges. The classical expression of wisdom is found in the Book of Proverbs.

The New Testament Christians inherited the wisdom

tradition from the Jews of the Old Testament era, just as they inherited the tradition of rules, and they employed the format of wisdom in order to describe the Christian way of life.

In the wisdom tradition, guidance for life does not take the form of commands; rather, it takes the form of shrewd advice about life. Here are some examples from Proverbs: "A gentle answer quiets anger" (Proverbs 15:1 TEV), "It is better to meet a mother bear robbed of her cubs than to meet some fool busy with a stupid project" (Proverbs 17:12 TEV), "Being cheerful keeps you healthy. It is slow death to be gloomy all the time" (Proverbs 17:22 TEV), "Enthusiasm without knowledge is not good" (Proverbs 19:2 TEV), and "When you give to the poor, it is like lending to the LORD, and the LORD will pay you back" (Proverbs 19:17 TEV).

Even though these passages contain no commands, they do contain specific guidance about how life is to be lived. In some ways the wisdom tradition is similar to the advice columns that we see in newspapers today, and people who want to live their lives well may turn to wisdom for guidance about how to do that.

In the New Testament the beatitudes of Jesus may be understood as wisdom:

Blessed are the poor in spirit, for theirs is the kingdom of heaven. Blessed are those who mourn, for they will be comforted. Blessed are the meek, for they will inherit the earth. Blessed are those who hunger and thirst for righteousness, for they will be filled. *Blessed are the merciful, for they will receive mercy. Blessed are the pure in heart, for they will see God. Blessed are the peacemakers, for they will be called children of God.*

—Matthew 5:3–9

These are not rules, but they provide guidance for our lives in the form of wise counsel. In his book, James used the form of wisdom to call his readers to Christian living:

All of us make many mistakes. Anyone who makes no mistakes in speaking is perfect.... How great a forest is set ablaze by a small fire! And the tongue is a fire.... Those conflicts and disputes among you, where do they come from? Do they not come from your cravings that are at war within you?... Are any among you suffering? They should pray. Are any cheerful? They should sing songs of praise.

—James 3:2, 5–6; 4:1; 5:13

James said, "If any of you is lacking in wisdom, ask God, who gives to all generously and ungrudgingly, and it will be given you" (James 1:5). Both rules and wisdom are helpful formats for the call to Christian living. But they are not the only formats.

VIRTUES
In the New Testament a third format for the call to Christian living is a list of virtues; several such lists

appear throughout the New Testament. Virtues are moral qualities that should characterize the lives of Christians. For example, in Galatians Paul wrote: "The fruit of the Spirit is love, joy, peace, patience, kindness, generosity, faithfulness, gentleness, and self-control" (Galatians 5:22–23). What we have here is neither rules nor wisdom, but a description of the kind of character Christians should have.

In Colossians Paul used the metaphor of changing clothes as a way to present vices and virtues: "You must get rid of all such things—anger, wrath, malice, slander, and abusive language….clothe yourselves with compassion, kindness, humility, meekness, and patience" (Colossians 3:8, 12). Paul did not explain *how* we are to put off the vices and put on the virtues, but he was certainly clear about which qualities are vices and which are virtues.

IMAGES

Many Christ followers today are familiar with rules, and some are familiar with wisdom and with virtues. In this book we are going to study another format in which the writers of the New Testament issued the call to Christian living, one that has received less attention than the others. That form is images of Christians.

Scattered through the New Testament are numerous images of Christians. For example, Jesus told His disciples, "I am the vine, you are the branches" (John 15:5). This striking image expresses beautifully that there is a very close relationship between Christ and Christians. It serves to remind us that, just as branches draw their life and nourishment from the vine, so Christians draw their life and nourishment from Christ; Christians must, like branches, remain in the vine in order to live and to bear fruit.

In order to keep this book a manageable length, I have restricted myself to personal images; for that reason I have not included images such as vines and branches (vines and branches aren't persons). Nor have I attempted to explore all of the personal images in the New Testament; for example, the writers of the New Testament sometimes spoke of Christians as farmers (2 Timothy 2:6), as citizens (Ephesians 2:19), and as ambassadors (2 Corinthians 5:20), but I have not included these images in this book.

THE CHRISTIAN AND THE CHURCH

The Christian way of life is wonderful; it is, in fact, the way that God always intended for human beings to live. But it also is a demanding way of life, so demanding that we cannot live it by ourselves.

In this book we will be giving attention to individual Christ followers: each of us is a disciple, a servant, a steward, and so on. Because our emphasis in this book is on individuals, I want to emphasize here, before we begin looking at the images, that it is not possible for us to live as Christians if we are isolated from all other Christians. To live as Christians, we must be in the church. You cannot live as a faithful Christian if you cut yourself off from all other Christians.

Let me explain why. From the beginning of the world, God was concerned to create a community of persons to be the people of God. When human beings fell into sin, they not only experienced alienation from God; they also experienced alienation from each other; the wars, racism, divorces, violence, and crime that characterize our world display the fact that alienation is still a problem for us in the twenty-first century.

Despite human sin, God continued to pursue that original purpose of creating a community of persons to be God's own people. By the Spirit, God has created a worldwide community of faith in Jesus, so that there is in our world today a people of God; this community, the church, comprises hundreds of millions of people. If we are to live as Christians, we must do so in fellowship not only with the Lord but also with this community of faith. No one can follow Christ privately; we do it in community.

Naturally we Christ followers relate to the community of faith in different ways, and that is all right; the important thing is that we not cut ourselves off from that community entirely. As we study these images of ourselves found in the New Testament, we shall refer regularly to the implications of the images for our participation in the life of the church.

IDENTITY AND CONDUCT

Our sense of personal identity is one of the most important things in all of our lives. How we think of ourselves and how we feel about ourselves are important because we tend to live in ways that are consonant with our thoughts and feelings about ourselves.

God's other creatures apparently live in ways that are determined completely by their identity; tigers always act like tigers, and water always acts like water.

For human beings, things are a little different. Though our conduct is not absolutely determined by our identity, as is the case with God's other creatures, our conduct is profoundly influenced by our identity. A good, clear sense of who we are helps us to live life more fully and appropriately.

Many factors make up our identity. For us Christians, a very important part of our identity is that we are, in fact, Christ followers. It is my hope that, as you and I reflect seriously on the biblical images of Christ followers, we may come to a richer understanding of what it means to be Christians, that is, that we will internalize more fully the truth that we are, in fact, disciples, servants, stewards, and so on. And, of course, we may also hope that as we come to grasp our identity better, we may also understand more fully the kind of life which God is calling us to live and, in so understanding, be helped to live it. As one of the finest writers on biblical images, Harriet Crabtree, has pointed out, "Images do have this formative power."[1]

In order for these things to happen, both the author and his readers need repeatedly to ask themselves this question: have I internalized as fully as possible the truth that I am a disciple, a servant, a steward, and so on? What does it mean for my life that I am in fact a disciple, a servant, a steward? As I was writing this book, I attempted to ask these questions of myself, and it was a good experience for me; I invite my readers to ask the same questions of themselves as they read the book.

"Follow me."

—Matthew 4:19

$\mathcal{D}$isciple

When Jesus lived on earth, Israel had several different kinds of religious leaders, including priests, prophets, and rabbis.

Priests led the people in worship and instructed them; you had to be born into the priesthood, by being a male in the tribe of Levi. Jesus was not born into the priesthood; He was born into the tribe of Judah rather than that of Levi.

There also were prophets in Israel, of whom the most famous by far was Jesus' relative, John the Baptist. In some ways Jesus

Himself was a prophet, though His ministry was quite different from John's. John seems to have spoken about political matters more than Jesus. Also, he seems to have addressed the nation as a whole, whereas Jesus often addressed His message to individual listeners.

And then there were rabbis. Rabbis were the teachers of the Jewish faith and way of life. Jesus was a rabbi, and He accepted that title when others used it of Him (for example, John 3:2). He did not teach in a particular town or synagogue, as modern rabbis do, but rather He carried out His teaching ministry as He moved around the towns and countryside of Galilee; He was an itinerant rabbi.

Jesus was different from most rabbis in other ways also. One of the things that characterized the ministry of rabbis was that they had disciples. These were young men who volunteered to be the rabbi's students and who learned the teachings of their rabbi, with a view to becoming rabbis themselves. Jesus did not wait for young men to volunteer to become His disciples. Rather, He took the initiative and called several men to follow Him. Moreover, He chose unlikely disciples, men who had families and who already were involved in other forms of work.

It was characteristic of rabbis that they devoted a great deal of attention to the Hebrew Scriptures, the Old Testament. Jesus was different in this regard also; except on occasion, He did not offer many comments on the Hebrew Scriptures, but instead He simply proclaimed His message. His listeners were struck by the authority with which He spoke His message in a straightforward way (see Mark 1:22).

Rabbis conventionally taught only males, and Jesus was different in this regard also, because He taught women. On one occasion when Jesus was visiting in the home of two sisters who were His friends, one of them, Martha, criticized her sister Mary for listening to Jesus rather than working in the kitchen. Behind Martha's criticism of Mary lay the conventional understanding that the teaching of rabbis was not for women. Jesus reprimanded her and told her that, in learning from Him, "Mary has chosen the better part, which will not be taken away from her" (Luke 10:42).

The novelist and short story writer, Isaac Singer, wrote a fascinating story about a young woman in Poland who was taught by her father, a rabbi, in secret, because women in Poland were not supposed to be taught the Torah. Entitled *Yentl*, it was made in 1983 into a movie starring Barbra Streisand. The theme was the same as in the story of Mary and Martha.

So, Jesus was an unusual rabbi. But He was a rabbi, He did have disciples, and He still does.

As you and I begin to reflect on the fact that we are disciples of rabbi Jesus, it will be helpful to keep in mind that when He was on earth Jesus had followers who were literally His disciples. You and I are really and truly Jesus' disciples; those men were literally His disciples. We will find some parallels between their lives and ours, but because we are not disciples in the literal way that they were, there are also some differences between their discipleship and ours. For example, one of the things that those first disciples had to do in order to follow rabbi Jesus was to leave their homes and families and travel around Israel with Jesus. Jesus does not call most of us today to travel because, of course, He is not physically present on earth now as He was then. He does call some of us, missionaries, to travel, but most of us live out our discipleship in our homes and with our families, not by leaving our homes and families.

In the Great Commission, Jesus told His disciples that they should make disciples of all nations (Matthew 28:19), which suggests that Jesus intended to be rabbi to many other people beside His original disciples. Therefore it is somewhat surprising to learn that only one writer of the New Testament used the word *disciples* to describe all Christians.[1] That writer was Luke, author of both Luke and Acts. So, for example, we read in Acts 6: "The disciples were increasing in number" (verse 1), "The twelve called together the whole community of the disciples" (verse 2), and "The number of the disciples increased greatly" (verse 7).

It is Luke, therefore, who makes it clear that it is appropriate for all Christians today to understand themselves as disciples of the rabbi Jesus.

APPRENTICES

Earlier I said that disciples are students who learn from their rabbi. However, I am not sure that it is a good idea to use the word *students* to describe Christian disciples. This word has connotations that may mislead us.

What do we today think of when we hear the word *students*? I think that, for most of us, students are people who have not yet gone out into the real world but rather are enrolled in institutions of learning where they are insulated from the outside world. They attend classes, listen to lectures, take notes, study books, write papers, and learn, all in an attempt to pass tests and to receive diplomas and degrees, so that they will be prepared to go out into the real world.

Understood in that sense, the word *students* does not give us an appropriate understanding of Christian disciples. Disciples of Jesus are already involved in the real world, not insulated from it. And, except for studying and learning, the other things done by today's students do not apply to Christian disciples.

I want to suggest, therefore, that it is more helpful to speak of Christ's disciples as apprentices of rabbi Jesus rather than as students of rabbi Jesus. You and I are apprenticed to our rabbi Jesus.

Apprentices are found in several sectors of modern life; for instance, there are apprentices in the building trades. At the beginning of their careers, young men, and sometimes young women, too, become apprentice carpenters, apprentice plumbers, apprentice electricians, and so on. In apprenticeships, as a rule, there are no classrooms, no lectures, no note-taking, no paper-writing, and no written tests.

Moreover, apprentice carpenters are not preparing to become carpenters; as the phrase *apprentice carpenters* makes clear, they already are carpenters; they are apprentices in order to learn how to become really good carpenters. That is true of those of us who are Jesus' disciples. We are already living our lives as Christians; while we are doing that, we also are learning from rabbi Jesus how to be really good Christians.

So, Christians are disciples of their rabbi Jesus who are learning from Him how to live their lives.

Now we face a question: do we in fact think that Jesus can teach us how our lives should be lived? We all believe that Jesus is our savior and Lord, but do we also think of Him as the master of life who is best able to teach us how to live? Only if we believe this will we have any incentive to apprentice ourselves to Him in order to learn how to live our lives.

One of our fine contemporary writers is convinced that the understanding that Jesus is the master of life is missing from much of the church today. Dallas Willard thinks that, though most Christians today believe in Jesus as the Son of God and as their savior, many of them do not really think of Jesus as "of vital relevance to the course of their actual lives."[2] Jesus is not their rabbi, so they are not His disciples. Willard's question to contemporary Christians is this:

Who teaches you? Whose disciple are you? Honestly.

One thing is sure: You are somebody's disciple. You learned how to live from somebody else. There are no exceptions to this rule, for human beings are just the kind of creatures that have to learn and keep learning from others how to live....

The assumption of Jesus' program for his people on earth was that they would live their lives as his students and co-laborers. They would find him so admirable in every respect—wise, beautiful, powerful, and good—that they would constantly seek to be in his presence and be guided, instructed, and helped by him in every aspect of their lives.[3]

As we think about being Jesus' disciples, we should ask ourselves this question: do I honestly believe that Jesus, better than anyone else, can teach me how I ought to live my life?

Luke, who taught us that Christians are disciples, also used another unique phrase to refer to Christians. He spoke of them as people who belonged to "the Way" (Acts 9:2, 19:23). The source of this phrase is unknown, but its meaning seems to include the idea that Christians are persons who live in a certain way—which, to the extent that they are good disciples of Jesus, they certainly do.

THE IMITATION OF CHRIST

Assuming we are prepared to learn about life from Jesus, how do we learn? We learn, I think, in pretty much the same way apprentices in the building trades learn, by observing master plumbers and master electricians and then imitating what they do. Just as an apprentice carpenter watches a master carpenter hang cabinets and imitates him, so we watch Jesus live and imitate Him. We learn by imitation.

Jesus called us to do this. He said, "If any want to become my followers, let them deny themselves and take up their cross and follow me" (Mark 8:34). Jesus was talking about being a giver and not just a taker in life, and He was prepared to be a giver even when that involved self-sacrifice. Christians imitate Jesus by doing the same thing.

Similarly, Jesus said, on the occasion when He served His disciples by washing their feet before they had their last supper with Him, "I have set you an example, that you also should do as I have done to you" (John 13:15). He meant that His disciples were to imitate His service to others.

The writers of the New Testament also spoke about the importance of imitating Christ. For example, Peter told his readers who were experiencing suffering in their lives, "Christ also suffered for you, leaving you an example, so that you should follow in his steps" (1 Peter 2:21). Jesus' disciples are to cope with the difficulties and sufferings of their lives in the same way Jesus coped with suffering in His life: without complaining, without retaliating, and with trust in God and obedience to God. That is what it means to walk "in his steps"; this phrase of Peter's became the title of a book by Charles M. Sheldon in which Christ followers were urged to ask themselves in every situation, *What would Jesus do?*

In his letter to the church at Philippi, Paul appealed to the example of Jesus. Paul's immediate concern was to help the church at Philippi be united in spirit and live at peace, and he believed that unity and peace depended upon the church members having humility, that is, having a bedrock, basic respect for each other. So he wrote to them: "Let the same mind be in you that was in Christ Jesus, who, though he was in the form of God, did not regard equality with God as something to be exploited, but emptied himself, taking the form of a slave, being born in human likeness" (Philippians 2:5–7). Good disciples of Jesus will have the same mind as Christ; they will imitate His extraordinary humility and so learn how life should be lived.

One of the most influential New Testament scholars of the twentieth century, C.H. Dodd, wrote this about the importance of imitating Christ:

The idea that man should imitate God, or should become as like God as possible, is a very widespread ethical conception. It was part of the preaching both of Greek moralists and of the teachers of Judaism. But it can be a very dangerous maxim. If you heard it said of someone that "he behaves like a little god," you would not take it for praise.... The counsel to imitate God, therefore, or to become like God, is one that we have to use with very great caution....

The New Testament idea of the imitation of Christ is a way of making explicit what kinds of divine activity should be imitated by men, and how, and why, and in what circumstances.... It is in respect of the love which Christ showed to man that the character and action of God are to be copies. To follow His steps is to have before us a truly human example, but it is also to have the divine pattern made comprehensible and imitable.[4]

Disciples of Christ study His life and reflect on it, because they must know about Him in order to learn to imitate Him. There is no end to this reflection; the life of Jesus remains for His disciples a limitless source of wisdom and inspiration for living.

INSTRUCTION

Of course, apprentices not only have the example of their mentors; they also receive instructions from them. For example, master carpenters explain to apprentice carpenters how to hang cabinets straight. The same is true of Christ. In addition to giving us His example, Jesus gave us instructions about how to live.

Jesus gave us so many instructions about life that it is impossible to review them all here. All that we can do is review a few of them briefly, doing so in the awareness that there is a lot more where these came from. We shall begin with some instructions from the Sermon on the Mount.

Our rabbi Jesus taught us that we are to put God's Kingdom ahead of everything else in life (Matthew 6:33).

God's Kingdom is God's rule over the lives of people; God extended the Kingdom over the lives of people through the life and work of Jesus. Putting God's Kingdom ahead of everything else in life means getting our priorities right. Nothing is more important than that God reign as God over the lives of human beings.

Our rabbi Jesus taught us that we should be peacemakers (Matthew 5:9). Our world is filled with violence, conflict, and war; the disciples of Jesus are not to contribute to the conflict, but rather to wage peace, beginning in their own homes and moving out into more distant venues.

Our rabbi Jesus taught us to hunger and thirst for righteousness (Matthew 5:6). It is natural for human beings to long for things in life, things ranging from the ordinary—for example, material possessions—to the sublime—for example, children. Jesus understood that we all long for things; it is to us, with all our longings, that Jesus said, *Your greatest longing should be to become a good person.* Every disciple of Christ should ask, *Along with everything else I long for, do I really hunger and thirst to become a better person?*

Our rabbi Jesus taught us to forgive our enemies and to pray for them (Matthew 5:43–48). Forgiving is one of the most difficult things Christians have to do. We naturally want to hit back at those who hurt us, but Jesus calls us to forgive them and to pray for them.

Our rabbi Jesus taught us that the two most important things we do in life are to love God and to love our neighbors

(Matthew 22:34–40). He didn't say these are the only things in life, but He did say they are the most important things. If we manage to achieve all other things but do not learn to love, our lives will have been wasted. If we learn to love God and our neighbors, we will have been successful, however much or little else we may have achieved.

These are just five of the instructions about life given to us by our rabbi Jesus. In the Gospels (and elsewhere too— see Acts 20:35, for example) are recorded dozens, perhaps hundreds, of Jesus' instructions about life. We who are apprenticed to Jesus study these instructions in order to learn how to live life as God intends it to be lived.

LEARNING BY DOING

So far, we have seen that we are apprenticed to Jesus to learn His way of life and that we learn by imitating Him and also by paying careful attention to His instructions.

Our next point is that we learn Jesus' way by putting it into practice. Just as apprentice carpenters learn carpentry by doing it, so we learn Jesus' way of life by doing it.

There are things in life that you can't learn just by hearing about them or reading about them. For example, you can read several books about bicycling, but if you don't get on a bicycle and try to ride it, you will never learn to ride a bicycle. The same is true of swimming, and of using a computer; you have to attempt to do these things in order to learn how to do them.

So it is with Jesus' way of life. You have to try to live it in order to learn it; no amount of abstract knowledge of Jesus' teachings can compare to simply doing what He said: make the Kingdom your priority, forgive your enemies, work for peace, and so on.

Incidentally, attempting to put Jesus' teachings into practice is one way of confirming that Jesus is the trustworthy rabbi and indeed the savior of human beings. We live in an age of science when some people have lost whatever faith in God they may once have had. Some of them are wistful about the faith they lost and wish they could somehow recover it. They are reluctant to live lives characterized by doubt concerning life's most important issues.

There are various strategies for helping them to recover their faith. One of the best is for them to attempt to put Jesus' teachings into practice: "Anyone who resolves to do the will of God will know whether [my] teaching is from God," Jesus said (John 7:17). If you are troubled by doubt, why not pray the Lord's Prayer, attempt to be a peacemaker, try to forgive your enemies, and then ask yourself, *Did Jesus know what He was talking about?* I think that you will find the answer to be, yes, He really did.

Today we use the word *praxis* to name the process of learning-by-doing. In order to learn while living, we need to reflect on our lives.

TIMES FOR REFLECTING
This leads us to ask, when do we reflect upon how we are living?

Sometimes we do our reflecting simultaneously with our living. Our reflection is immediate and spontaneous, and we learn from that. We learn what to do and what not to do by being attentive to what happens when we behave in certain ways.

Self-reflection is important for disciples of Jesus. We can't lurch through life thoughtlessly and be very good disciples. We need to cultivate attentiveness to how we are living, always asking if the ways we are living are truly Jesus' ways.

Reflecting as we move through life is valuable, but it is not enough. In order to be the best disciples we can be, we need to set aside times for a more systematic reflection on our lives than is possible in the rush of life.

That is one of the reasons we have devotional practices. We study the Bible and think about what it says to us about Jesus and His way of life. We pray to God about things that are happening in our lives. Perhaps we keep a journal in which we record and interpret events in our lives. Devotional practices such as these help us to do the sort of reflection that apprentices need to do in order to learn their craft.

Both reflecting as we live and reflecting in devotional practices are important. But both are private; we do them solo. We also need to practice reflection in the company of other disciples.

Earlier I mentioned that it was Luke who referred to all Christians as disciples. He did so 30 times in the Book of

Acts. Three of these usages are of individual disciples; the other 27 usages are in the plural, referring to the community of disciples, not to individual disciples.

This makes it clear that, if we want to think of disciples in the biblical way, we must think of a community of disciples. And this means that the community needs to reflect together on what Jesus' way of life is and on how well they are living it.

The church should be a forum in which we disciples reflect together on our lives in light of what we know about Jesus and His way of life. We meet together in order to, among other things, learn His way of life and consider how well we are living it. In the church we engage in a complex and ongoing conversation about discipleship. Through hymns and Bible studies, and on mission trips, and, yes, in sermons and in the reading of Scripture, and in prayer, and in informal conversations with fellow Christians, we are engaged in *praxis*, a process of learning-by-doing the way of life of Jesus.

The church is the only large face-to-face community of moral discourse in which most of us are ever engaged. Certainly the church in the aggregate is the largest community of moral discourse here in the United States.

Here, in the fellowship of those on the Way, we ask ourselves: am I behaving as a good Christian parent? As a good Christian employer? As a good Christian citizen? The way of Jesus is good, but we can't be good disciples if we attempt to fly solo.

BARRIERS TO DISCIPLESHIP

Four things can prevent us from being good disciples. First, we may not have the information we need. Many Christians know a great deal less about Jesus' example and instructions than they need to know. Sometimes we simply need to read the Gospels and to pay attention to what is said there.

Paying attention can be difficult, because there is always a tendency in the church to domesticate the message of Jesus, and another tendency to pay attention to some of Jesus' teachings while ignoring others. It takes prayer and discipline to be really attentive to what Jesus is telling us about how to live our lives.

For example, Jesus said that it is very difficult for rich people to enter the Kingdom (Matthew 19:16–26). By the standards of the past and by the standards of most of the people in the world today, we Americans are rich. How can we use our possessions rather than become enslaved to them? It won't be easy—Jesus said it wouldn't. He didn't say it was impossible, but He did say it was difficult. We need to pay attention to what He said, and not domesticate it.

We overcome the first barrier to living as disciples by getting a fuller and better understanding of Jesus' way of life.

The second barrier for many of us is that we have become teachers ourselves. When you are a teacher, it's difficult to remember that you are also still a learner. I have been a Christian teacher for four decades; I find it hard to remember that, when it comes to Jesus' way of life, I am still a disciple, an apprentice. I have to remind myself intentionally that there is only one Master of this way of life, and that I will always be learning from Him.

A third barrier for American Christians is that we live in a society and culture in which we expect to get things done quickly. Our context bewitches us into thinking that it is possible to get a quick fix on Jesus' way.

We can't. It takes time to understand all that Jesus calls us to be, and it takes time for us to become the kinds of persons who naturally want to live Jesus' way. We can get our dry cleaning done quickly and our photographs developed quickly and our lunch served quickly, but we can't become strong and courageous and wise Christians quickly. It takes time. In fact, it takes a lifetime. It's like a marriage; you have to devote your entire life to getting it right.

A fourth barrier to discipleship is that we don't devote ourselves enthusiastically to it. Many of us live busy lives, and we would like to think of Christian discipleship as one more thing that we can add on top of all the other things that are already important to us and to which we are already devoted. So we don't hunger and thirst for righteousness as much as we hunger and thirst for comfort, and we don't seek God's Kingdom first because what we seek first is the happiness of our families.

Part of being a serious disciple of Jesus is to recognize

the deep ambiguities of our own hearts, and to learn to see through our rationalizations. We must keep working through this process honestly until we can say with passion, *Lord, I want to be like Jesus, in my heart.*

CONCLUSION

You and I will never drift thoughtlessly into Christian discipleship. We have to commit ourselves to it intentionally. The challenge today is just what it was long ago. Here is what Albert Schweitzer, one of the great missionary doctors of the twentieth century, said about Jesus' call to us:

He comes to us as One unknown, without a name, as of old, by the lake-side, He came to those men who knew Him not. He speaks to us the same word: "Follow thou me!" and sets us to the tasks which he has to fulfill for our time. He commands. And to those who obey Him, whether they be wise or simple, He will reveal Himself in the toils, the conflicts, the sufferings which they shall pass through in His fellowship, and, as an ineffable mystery, they shall learn in their own experience Who He is. [5]

As we live Jesus' way, we learn who He is. We also learn who we are, and what from the beginning God intended for us to be. Dietrich Bonhoeffer, one of the German Christians who resisted Hitler, wrote this:

And if we answer the call to discipleship, where will it lead us? What decisions and partings will it demand? To answer this question we shall have to go to him, for only he knows the answer. Only Jesus Christ, who bids us follow him, knows the journey's end. But we do know that it will be a road of boundless mercy. Discipleship means joy.[6]

As disciples of Christ, we are apprenticed to Him, committed to the way of life He lived and taught, and learning that way by reflecting on it as we attempt to live it.

CHAPTER 2

*"His servants
shall serve him."*

—Revelation 22:3 KJV

Servant

In the New Testament there is only one word (*mathetes*) for disciples, but there are three words for servants. In a basic sense, "to serve" is *diakonein*; our English word *deacon* comes from this. "To serve" in the sense of being a slave is *douleuein*. "To serve" in the sense of offering reverence is *latreuein*. All three words, in both their noun and verb forms, are used of Christians. We are servants, slaves, and worshipers of God.

This understanding of ourselves creates difficulties for twenty-first century Christians. None of us owns slaves, and we find the institution of

51

slavery morally repugnant. Few of us have servants, and most of us would feel uncomfortable if we did; we also would feel uncomfortable thinking of ourselves as someone else's servant.

In our minds, servanthood and slavery are demeaning. To be a servant is to be without dignity; to be a slave is to be without either dignity or freedom. Freedom and dignity are two of the qualities we prize most highly today.

It is not just in our modern world that people have felt uncomfortable about being servants or slaves; there are some hints that already in the era of the New Testament the church had some reservations about these terms. For example, Jesus said to His disciples, "I do not call you servants any longer" (John 15:15). Paul wrote to the Romans, "You did not receive a spirit of slavery to fall back into fear" (Romans 8:15), and to the Galatians, "You are no longer a slave but a child" (Galatians 4:7). It sounds in these passages as if the writer felt some discomfort with the images of servants or slaves.

Nevertheless, the images of servant and slave are frequently used in the New Testament, and that presents us with the question of how to understand them in a way that does not diminish us.

One possibility is to ignore the problem. In our discussion of discipleship we were able to ignore the fact that, though Jesus' original disciples had to leave their families in order to follow Him, we do not have to do that.

But the problem with servant and slave is a little different because, whereas discipleship does not necessarily require travel, slavery seems necessarily to deny freedom and dignity.

A second possibility is to translate the words *servant* and *slave* into approximate modern equivalents that do not carry demeaning connotations. For example, we could say that we are employees of God or members of God's staff, and that we work in God's world for God. Up to a point, this is helpful. It certainly eliminates the troubling connotations of slavery; employees are not necessarily diminished by their work, and many of them are proud of their work and of the institutions with which they are associated in their work. I, for example, am very pleased to have served as a faculty member at Samford University for the past fifteen years.

On the other hand, these modern images have liabilities of their own. For example, there are many good employers today, whereas the early Christians were strongly committed to the idea that there is only one good Lord. Also, many employees today do not really care about their work but do it only for pay (fortunately, this is not true of everyone), and this could suggest that God's servants do their work only for pay, which would be very misleading.

A third way to deal with the problem is to argue that, whether we realize it or not, all of us are enslaved to someone or something. The question is not whether we are slaves; we all are. The question is, who is your master?

The apostle Paul was doing something like this when he told the Romans, "You have been set free from sin and are the slaves of God" (Romans 6:22 TEV).

Recently one scholar has argued that in the Roman world slaves could rise to managerial work and could receive respect if their masters were persons of high social status; from this he arrived at the following conclusion about Paul's speaking of himself as Christ's slave: "Surprising as it may seem to modern readers, Paul's slavery to Christ did not connote humility but rather established his authority as Christ's agent and spokesperson."[1]

Across the centuries many Christians have dealt in this way with the relationship between our being free and our being slaves: they have asserted that to experience slavery to God rather than to sin or death is to experience freedom and dignity.

Our conclusion is that all human beings have freedom and dignity because they have been created in the image of God, and for that reason they should all be treated with respect. Our freedom and dignity have been damaged by the fact that we have sinned, and, in a sense, we have forfeited our full freedom and dignity by becoming slaves to sin. When we became Christians, we were delivered from that slavery and restored to our full freedom and dignity before God, who is now our true Lord and Master in a way that preserves rather than diminishes our freedom and dignity.

WHOM WE SERVE

Sometimes in the New Testament Christians are said to be servants of God. For example, Paul said that he was "a servant of God" (Titus 1:1), and he said that offering our lives to God is an act of service to God (Romans 12:1).

Much more frequently, however, Christians are said to be servants of Jesus. Every time we make the most basic of all Christian confessions, that Jesus is Lord, we are in fact acknowledging that we are His servants. Jude (1:1), Peter (2 Peter 1:1), and Paul (Romans 1:1, Philippians 1:1) all spoke of themselves as servants of Jesus. In a prayer meeting in Jerusalem, Christians prayed: "And now, Lord,...grant to your servants to speak your word with all boldness" (Acts 4:29). Paul reminded the church leaders at Ephesus that he had come to them "serving the Lord with all humility" (Acts 20:19). To the church at Rome he said simply, "Serve the Lord" (Romans 12:11), and he assured them that "The one who thus serves Christ is acceptable to God and has human approval" (Romans 14:18).

The language about servants and their service to Christ appears throughout the New Testament. Jesus had employed this kind of language Himself; for example, He alerted His followers that no one can serve two masters (Matthew 6:24), and in several of His parables God's people occupy the role of servants of God.

James combined the ideas of serving God and serving Jesus when he described himself as follows: "James, a servant of God and of the Lord Jesus Christ" (James 1:1).

So, we Christians are servants of God and servants of Jesus Christ. Jesus is our Lord and Master, and the church is a team of fellow-servants.

JESUS, THE SERVANT OF THE LORD

So far, things seem pretty simple, but there is more to be said. For, of course, Jesus Himself is not only our Lord; He also was Himself a servant of God. He told His followers that He came into the world to do His Father's work (John 4:34) and that He had not come from heaven to do His own will but the will of the Father (John 6:38).

His Father's work was, of course, the salvation of human beings. And this means that, in a true sense, Jesus came into the world to serve the Father by serving the spiritual needs of human beings.

On one occasion Jesus' followers became embroiled in a heated argument about which of them would be closest to Jesus when the Kingdom of God fully arrived. Jesus used this argument as an occasion to turn their value system upside down and to teach them about the meaning of their lives: "Whoever wishes to be great among you must be your servant, and whoever wishes to be first among you must be your slave; just as the Son of Man [this is Jesus' favorite self-designation] came not to be served but to serve, and to give his life a ransom for many" (Matthew 20:26–28).

Jesus served God by devoting His life to the service of other people, and His followers are to do the same. So, in a true sense, Christians are not only servants of Jesus, but also servants of other people. Paul wrote, "I have made myself a slave to all," and he told his readers to do the same: "Through love become slaves to one another" (1 Corinthians 9:19, Galatians 5:13). He was talking about serving people because we love them and care about their welfare.

GOD DOES NOT NEED OUR SERVICE

This helps to explain one of the most puzzling things about being God's servants, namely, that we cannot imagine that God would have any need of servants. In "On His Blindness" the Puritan poet John Milton wrote that "God doth not need...man's work. Thousands at his bidding speed,"[2] and he was right. Surely whatever God wants done can be effected simply by God's speaking it; after all, that is how God created the world. What need, then, does God have of human servants?

Of course the answer is, no need at all. Christians are not God's servants in the sense that God has needs that we are to try to meet. We are God's servants in that God's world has needs that we are to try to meet, and as we do that, we serve God.

The author of Proverbs put this in a charming way: "When you give to the poor, it is like lending to the LORD, and the LORD will pay you back" (19:17 TEV). Jesus elaborated the same idea in Matthew 25, when He taught that at the final judgment He will tell some people that they may enter the Kingdom because they fed Him when He was hungry and they clothed Him when He was naked. They are baffled by this; they don't remember helping Him in these ways. He says to them, "Truly I tell you, just as you did it to one of the least of these who are members of my family, you did it to me" (Matthew 25:40).

This is a principle by which we all should live. In the sixteenth century the German reformer Martin Luther wrote a book entitled *The Freedom of a Christian* in which he defended two propositions: "A Christian is a perfectly free lord of all, subject to none. A Christian is a perfectly dutiful servant of all, subject to all."[3] Luther was fully aware that his statements were paradoxical, but he insisted that both of them are in fact true, and he reminded his listeners that the apostle Paul had taught the same thing when he wrote that, "Though I am free with respect to all, I have made myself a slave to all" (1 Corinthians 9:19).

In the twentieth century, Mother Teresa of Calcutta carried out her entire life's work on the principle of treating each one of the poorest of the poor of Calcutta as if that one were Jesus.

Martin Luther and Mother Teresa understood Christian service well. Christians are not ashamed to think of themselves as servants of God; rather we are thankful that God is our Lord and Master. Though we are free people, we have freely chosen to be servants of God. Following Jesus' example, we attempt not to be served but to serve others, and to do so as our way of serving our God, who does not need our service.

OBEDIENCE: FORGIVENESS

Each of the images of a Christian tells us particular things about our lives. It seems to me that the image of servant tells us three things.

First, servants are obedient to their masters. We have been tough-minded about being Christ's servants; now we must be tough-minded about the fact that we are to live lives of obedience. We have many options in our lives, and many decisions to make, but there are some issues concerning which our only choice is obedience or disobedience to the Lord.

We will consider just one command of Jesus. Jesus has taught His servants how to treat their enemies. We are not to retaliate but to pray for our enemies and to forgive them: "Love your enemies and pray for those who persecute you" (see Matthew 5:43–48, 6:9–15, and 18:23–35). What does it mean to obey this command of Jesus?

The best way to describe forgiveness is not by definition but by narrative. It begins when someone does something that hurts you. It may be a group, or an individual. It may be someone in your family, or a friend. It may be someone you work with, or someone you work for, or someone who works for you. For some Christ followers it has been a group or an individual in a church somewhere.

Those who hurt you may have intended to do so, but sometimes they didn't; nevertheless, you were hurt. Sometimes those who hurt you aren't even aware of the pain they have caused you. Nevertheless, you were hurt.

You don't deserve the pain they caused you. You aren't perfect, but nothing you have done warrants this. In short, it's unfair, unjust.

How do you respond to being hurt deeply and unfairly? Jesus commands you to forgive. But what does that mean?

Forgiveness means suffering in a special way. In order to forgive, you have to accept two kinds of pain. First comes the pain of being treated unfairly. In this world, all of us experience that kind of pain, and there's no way to avoid it.

In forgiveness there is another kind of pain also. When you're treated unfairly, you become angry. No one has to learn to do this; it is a natural instinct. Even small children feel it. Because you are angry, you naturally want to retaliate. This is an instinct also, and we all have it. We want to hit back. We want to hurt those who hurt us. You are entitled to want to retaliate. It's only fair. An eye for an eye, a tooth for a tooth. That balances the scales. That's justice.

But it's not forgiveness.

In forgiveness you voluntarily embrace the pain of your own anger rather than expressing it by means of retaliation. You absorb your anger. You don't repress or deny it; you live into it, and you live through it, in such a way as to drain the poison off it.

That's what forgiveness is: absorbing the pain caused by people who hurt you, and also absorbing the anger you naturally feel because you have been hurt. You do this in such a way as to neutralize it and so to end its destructive power in your life and in the lives of others.

I want to tell you that this is not fair. You didn't hurt the other person; the other person hurt you. You shouldn't have to suffer; the person who hurt you should have to suffer. But in the real world of moral relationships, it is the injured party who alone can forgive, and that means that it's the injured person who must suffer.

Forgiveness is very hard. But it is possible. Nelson Mandela was imprisoned in South Africa for more than a quarter of a century by a government that officially sponsored apartheid. One of that government's leaders was F. W. de Klerk. When Mandela was finally released from prison, he paid a visit to India, where he has many admirers. On one occasion an Indian official said to him, "I will be praying for your health." Mandela replied, "Thank you. Please pray also for the health of de Klerk."[4]

That cannot have been easy. But it is what Jesus calls His followers to do. We must forgive.

We often hear the phrase, "Forgive and forget," but, in fact, forgiveness is not forgetting. When you forgive, you remember that you were treated unfairly.

Forgiveness is not making excuses for the person who hurt you. In order to forgive you must not make excuses; you must be realistic about the fact that the other person wronged and hurt you.

Forgiveness isn't pretending that what happened to you doesn't matter. It does matter. That's why you have to deal with it even though it's difficult to do so.

Forgiveness is not always a single event. Often it is a process, and it can be a long process.

Because genuine forgiveness is difficult, we need a lot of help if we're going to do it. One thing that helps is simply to decide, intentionally, that you want to forgive. Not everyone wants to forgive. The natural response to being hurt is to retaliate; forgiveness is a response we have to make intentionally, and it is a painful response.

Another thing that helps is to belong to a community that supports you as you attempt to do it. The church is such a community. Other communities may support you in your natural inclination to get revenge, but the church is here to support you in the difficult work of forgiving your enemies.

It also helps to try to understand the person who hurt you. Maybe you can see why she acted the way she did. Maybe she's been hurt herself. Maybe she's having a lot of problems right now. You don't excuse her, but you do try to understand her, to see her humanity, and so not demonize her. In order to forgive, it helps to realize the humanity of the other person.

It helps to think about the future. Think about what will happen if you don't forgive and what will happen if you do. If you don't forgive, you'll continue to live with your anger, rage, and resentment. And you know what that will do. It will eat you up. It may make you physically ill; you can get hypertension, ulcers, headaches, insomnia, and rashes from bottling up your anger and from carrying resentment with you all the time. It will make you miserable not to forgive.

And not just you—others, too. If the world lives by the principle of an eye for an eye, it will soon be a world full of blind people. We pass along to others the hurts we have experienced ourselves.

On the other hand, if you do forgive, you will neutralize the pain that is destructive of your health and happiness. Then you can begin to experience healing. In this important sense, forgiveness is something you need to do for yourself.

There also is a chance that you and the person who hurt you may become friends again instead of enemies. That doesn't always happen, but at least there is a chance. In any case, you can do your part to make that happen.

In our lifetimes we have seen a dramatic public example of forgiveness, namely, the Truth and Reconciliation Committee of South Africa. The work of this group has been beautifully described by its most famous member, Bishop Desmond Tutu, in his book *No Future Without Forgiveness*. Tutu intended the title in the most literal sense; he believes that South Africa had no hope for a decent future unless it as a nation offered forgiveness to those who during the awful years of apartheid committed racist crimes. Without forgiveness, the nation would have begun an unending cycle of violence and retaliation. Thinking about that kind of future helps us to forgive.

Finally, it also helps to think about God. In one way or

another we have all hurt God. We haven't respected God as God, and we haven't put God first in our lives. We have mistreated people whom God loves. Nevertheless, God has forgiven us. In the sufferings of Jesus on the cross God absorbed and neutralized the pain that we caused Him. Forgiveness was difficult for God just as it is for us. There's always a price to be paid. It is because God has forgiven us that God is in a position to call on us to forgive those who hurt us.

I have been saying that forgiveness is difficult. Fortunately, there are some small, practical steps you can take that will move you toward the great task of forgiveness.

First, you can name the person or group who hurt you. You cannot begin to forgive until you acknowledge honestly that you have enemies who have hurt you.

In the South, where I live, this can be difficult to do, because we Southerners like to think that we don't have any enemies. I like to think that at my funeral the minister will be able to say, "Fisher didn't have an enemy in the world."

But we do have enemies. We all do. And if we are going to forgive them, we must begin by naming them and by naming the ways they have hurt us. You can't forgive generically.

Second, you can live in such a way as to do your enemies no harm. You can refuse to believe the worst things about them. You can refuse to be rude to them, and you can refuse to talk about them behind their backs. Talking about our enemies is one of the principal ways we retaliate; another is to withdraw and to be cool.

Third, you can refuse to stoke the fires of your anger. You don't replay the events in which you were mistreated and hurt; you don't mull them over. If you find that you cannot avoid thinking obsessively about those events and about the people who hurt you, you probably should talk to a friend who will understand you; that can help you move beyond being stuck on those things. In the event that doesn't do the job, you may need to get help from a pastor or other person who has been trained as a professional counselor; counselors understand our obsessions with those who have hurt us and can help us move beyond those feelings.

Fourth, you can pray for God to help you to forgive them. God wants you to forgive, so I think you can count on God to help you.

Fifth, you can begin to pray for your enemies. You should always do this privately; if you do it publicly, you will be tempted to be insincere. In the privacy of your heart, pray for your enemy. Perhaps at first you can't sincerely pray for your enemy's welfare; if not, restrict yourself to a prayer that is sincere. For example, you may say simply, "Lord, in obedience to Your command that we are to pray for our enemies, I pray for this person." If you will continue to do this, eventually the time will come when you will say, "Lord, in obedience to Your command that we pray for our enemies, I ask You to bless this person." When that happens, when you sincerely wish your enemy well, then you have forgiven your enemy.

Even so, your desire to retaliate may reassert itself later; don't be surprised if it does. Simply return to a sincere prayer for your enemy. (And, of course, if you yielded to the urge to retaliate, ask God to forgive you for that.)

Finally, you can be patient. Sometimes forgiveness is a slow process, but it's worth waiting for. The important thing is to begin to do it, to set the process of forgiveness in motion.

I want to mention one other matter about forgiveness, because it is a very important matter for anyone who attempts to obey Jesus' command to forgive. I have written here as if being hurt is a single, discrete event, and sometimes it is. However, there is also another way of being hurt that is not a single, discrete event but a continuing process, a pattern of being hurt. Today we have a word for that; we call it *abuse*.

Our Christian faith calls us to forgive. It does not call us to continue to accept abuse. If a pattern of abuse occurs, you should normally take steps to escape from it. Jesus' words in this regard are very important: "No one takes my life away from me. I give it up of my own free will. I have the right to give it up, and I have the right to take it back" (John 10:18 TEV). I think the same thing is true of ourselves.

Why have so many Christians thought that they are not supposed to try to get out of harm's way? One reason is simply that they think that the call to forgive is also a call to accept abuse; I think that's a mistaken assumption. Another reason is that Jesus said the following: "Do not resist an evildoer. But if anyone strikes you on the right cheek, turn the other also; and if anyone wants to sue you and take your coat, give your cloak as well; and if anyone forces you to go one mile, go also the second mile" (Matthew 5:39–41). I think that, in order to understand why Jesus said this, we must remember that His nation was then occupied by Roman soldiers who abused the people of Israel, and there was no way for the people to get out of harm's way. Jesus was counseling them, in their particular circumstances, not to attempt to resist the abuse, which would have involved violence and revolution; instead, He was saying, use the moral force of shaming the soldiers by giving them more than they ask for. Jesus was teaching people to resist evildoers by non-violence rather than by violence; He was not teaching them that it was wrong simply to get out of harm's way when that is possible.

There may be occasions when you will choose not to take yourself out of harm's way, but these occasions are, I believe, rare, and you need to be very clear in your own mind about why they are so exceptional that you will choose to continue to accept abuse.

Jesus commanded His servants to forgive their enemies, and we who are His servants must work hard to be obedient to His command. Needless to say, Jesus gave us many other commands as well.

WORK

Second, servants must work. Like obedience, work is obviously part of the role of servants.

It is striking how many Christians do not seem to realize that they are called to work. There is no way to be a good servant of Jesus without working hard (we have to work smart, too, as we will see in the next chapter). If I do not work at serving others as my way of serving Jesus, then I am being a poor servant.

In order to work, we can't just drift along in life and wait for people around us to tell us their needs. We must train ourselves to be alert to those needs. We must learn to listen between the lines of what people say to us, so that we can pick up on needs that they express indirectly rather than directly.

The ways we serve others usually depend on two factors. One is the particular needs of those whose lives we touch. In a wealthy community, our church probably doesn't need to sponsor a soup kitchen, but we may need to sponsor a branch of Alcoholics Anonymous. We must understand the needs of those around us, and then we must work to address their needs.

We also have to take into account our resources, such as spiritual gifts and money, and we should commit ourselves to those forms of service for which God has provided us resources. We ought also not to feel guilty if we lack the gifts to address certain needs. On the other hand, most people are able to do more than they realize they can, and most churches, if they will organize and devote themselves to things, are able to do much more service than they realize.

ACCOUNTABILITY

Third and finally, as servants of Christ we are accountable to God for how we live our lives. God is evaluating our service every day, and there will be a final assessment at the end. Christians should not be terrified about the final judgment, but they should be serious about it. Each of us is to live in such a way that at the end of our lives the Lord can say to us, "Well done, good and trustworthy slave; you have been trustworthy in a few things, I will put you in charge of many things; enter into the joy of your master" (Matthew 25:21).

CONCLUSION

Christ followers find true dignity and freedom in the service of the Lord. We are called to be obedient and to work hard, knowing that we are accountable to the Lord. Nothing is more fulfilling to us than to believe that by our service we have contributed something worthwhile to others and to God's work in the world.

In 1965 my wife Caroline and I met a lovely couple named Nancy and Peter Macky. At that time Peter and I were in graduate school together, and afterwards the Mackys and we settled in different parts of the country. Across the years since then we have seen each other occasionally, and we have kept in touch annually with Christmas cards and letters. Nancy has had a wonderful career teaching drama and related subjects in a college in Pennsylvania, and Peter has had a fine career as a teacher of New Testament in the same college; over the years Peter has written several fine books on a variety of subjects.

In 1996 Caroline and I received an extraordinary Christmas letter from Peter on behalf of himself and Nancy. It is the most moving account I have ever read of the experience that he and Nancy were then going through and which, sooner or later, all of us will go through. Here is part of the letter:

Our celebration of Christmas this year has been more poignant than usual, as we found in the backs of our minds the possibility that this could be our last one together. My diagnosis of mesothelioma, cancer of the lining of the lung (caused by asbestos, perhaps from the college chapel ceiling) puts a statistical limit on the length of time I probably have—another year on average. That does not take into consideration God's power to heal, for which we continue to pray, nor the possibility that the new experimental therapy (for which we are still waiting) may be highly effective. So we hope for the best, but have made most of the necessary plans for the worst.

Our basic attitude is that we are happy to be alive, happy to have each other and our children [they have two wonderful adult sons], happy to have our work in which we find fulfillment because we believe we are contributing to God's work on earth.

Thus we are taking all good things as great presents from God, especially this Christmas in which we celebrate the birth of Christ our Lord and Savior who has bound us together as a family, and as a community with many of you. (I have been wondering whether the angels celebrate Christmas, and if so when. In eternity there probably is no distinction of days, so perhaps there it is always Christmas, and always Easter.)

I have not been tempted by the Why me? black hole, for my view is that Ecclesiastes was right, that time and chance happen to all (Ecclesiastes 9:11), as Jesus also implied in saying God sends the sun and the rain indiscriminately on good and evil (Matthew 5:45). So there is no one to blame, certainly not God, for my bad luck. At the same time, however, we recognize that God has been wondrously good to us over many decades, and that we have far more to rejoice in than to regret. Most of all we rejoice in our life together, empowered as it is by the love of God which has come to us in Christ.

Peter died a few weeks after he wrote this letter.

Everything that Peter wrote in the letter seems true and important to me. Right now my concern is for his comment that he and Nancy were "happy to have our work in which we find fulfillment because we believe we are contributing to God's work on earth." In these words Peter expressed clearly why those of us who are servants and slaves of the Lord Jesus believe that we have a dignity and a freedom that is not available to those who do not attempt to serve the Lord. Our service to God is fulfilling to us because God uses it for important purposes.

As difficult as it is to admit it, we are all mortal; our lives on earth will one day come to an end. This naturally leads us to ask, *Is there anything that I can do that can make a difference beyond my own lifetime? Can I do anything of lasting importance?*

The answer is that we can. Our service, however great or small it may be, will be incorporated into the vast project by which God carries out the divine purposes for the world. To know that God will put our service to such grand use is indeed, as Peter wrote, to experience happiness. That is one reason that God's servants "serve the LORD with gladness" (Psalm 100:2 KJV).

CHAPTER 3

"Think of us…as…stewards of God's mysteries."

—1 Corinthians 4:1

Steward

Recently a friend told me a story about something that had happened in her Sunday school class. One Sunday the lesson was about being stewards, and the high school youth in her class did not seem to be getting the point, so she began to ask them questions. It turned out that the problem was that none of the youth had ever seen a steward or heard anyone today referred to as a steward.

This is understandable. A few years ago we had stewards and stewardesses on airplanes, but today those people are called *flight attendants*. Most of us have no occasion to use the word *steward* to refer to anyone living today.

So a study of the image of steward should begin by stating clearly what a steward is. A contemporary theologian has summarized the understanding of steward found in the Old Testament as follows: "The steward is one who has been given the responsibility for the management and service of something belonging to another, and his office presupposes a particular kind of trust on the part of the owner or master."[1]

Two of Jesus' parables confirm that this understanding was still operative in the New Testament era. In one (see Matthew 20:1–16) Jesus told about a man who owned a vineyard and hired day-laborers to work for him. The parable also contains a reference to a steward, a man who stood, so to speak, in between the owner and the workers. He was not the owner of the vineyard, but one of the servants; however, unlike the other servants, who simply worked, he had major responsibilities for the operation of the vineyard. In another parable (Luke 16:1–13) Jesus told about a businessman who had a steward who managed the affairs of the business so shrewdly that the businessman praised him.

In these parables it is evident that a steward is a manager who stands midway between the owner and the workers. The steward doesn't own the business, but the owner entrusts the business to the steward, and the owner expects the steward to manage the business wisely. A steward also is a supervisor who oversees the work of other servants in the business.

Sometimes what stewards manage is not a business but a household, and, in fact, the word for steward, *oikonomos*, contains the word for household, *oikos*. It also contains the word *nomos*, which means law or order, the idea being that a steward is someone who brings order into a household. Stewards may be responsible for things as varied as paying the other servants (see Matthew 20:8), treating the other servants properly in the owner's absence (see Luke 12:42–46), overseeing a wedding (see John 2:8–9), and educating children (see Galatians 4:1–2).

We usually associate stewardship with money, and that it understandable. In fact, our English word *economy* is derived from the Greek word *oikonomos*. In Romans Paul refers in passing to a man named Erastus who was the steward of a city, that is, a city treasurer (Romans 16:23). But though the association of stewardship with money is appropriate, as we shall see in a moment, there is a lot more to our being stewards than money.

OUR STEWARDSHIP

Let us begin our exploration of our stewardship with three observations. First, even when they did not employ the word *steward*, the writers of the New Testament were sometimes thinking of Christians as God's stewards. This is because all of the writers of the New Testament believe that God created everything that exists, including ourselves. God has redeemed us and given us new life; in that sense, God is the owner of our lives, and our lives have been entrusted to us by God. Therefore we should not think of ourselves so much as owners of things but rather as having been entrusted with whatever we have, and as being held responsible by God for our management of everything that God has entrusted to us. In this sense, our stewardship is being talked about in numerous passages in the New Testament writings where the word *steward* does not appear.

Second, there are two passages in which church leaders are explicitly described as stewards. In Titus 1:7 Paul provided a description of how bishops in the church are to live, and he says that they should live this way because they are stewards of God. The idea is that they are to be managers of the church's life and work.

Paul was more elaborate in his second reference to church leaders as stewards; it is found in his first letter to the church at Corinth. Speaking both of himself and of other church leaders, he wrote: "Think of us in this way, as servants of Christ and stewards of God's mysteries. Moreover, it is required of stewards that they be found trustworthy" (1 Corinthians 4:1–2).

"God's mysteries" are the truths of the gospel that have been entrusted by God to the church and its leaders. Paul felt a sense of responsibility for what the church does with the message of God's love given in Jesus Christ; he believed that God expected the church to manage wisely the proclamation of the gospel and the living out of its implications.

Third and finally, there is a passage in which Peter spoke about the stewardship of all Christians:

Like good stewards of the manifold grace of God, serve one another with whatever gift each of you has received. Whoever speaks must do so as one speaking the very words of God; whoever serves must do so with the strength that God supplies, so that God may be glorified in all things through Jesus Christ. To him belong the glory and the power forever and ever. Amen.

—1 Peter 4:10–11

In summary, there is a general sense in which our stewardship is assumed throughout the New Testament: we are not owners of our lives, but stewards of them. There is a specific sense in which the church and its leaders are stewards of the gospel message. And there is an additional specific sense in which every Christ follower is a steward of whatever gifts God has given her or him.

TWO MISTAKEN IDEAS

In order to understand ourselves as managers, we must deliberately set aside two mistaken ideas. One is the idea that we own our own lives; the other is the idea that all that God wants from us is unthinking obedience.

We do not own our lives; God owns them. God has created us ("It is he that made us, and we are his," Psalm 100:3), and God has redeemed us ("You are not your own...you were bought with a price," 1 Corinthians 6:20). In a true sense, then, everything that we think of as ours is really God's: our possessions, our families, our work. The image of steward teaches us that life and all that goes with it is a gift to us from God.

When we forget that everything we are and have is a gift from God, we set in motion destructive forces of possessiveness and control. It would probably be helpful to most of us to begin each day by saying to ourselves, "You are not your own. You were bought with a price." That might help us to accept the responsibility of living our lives in a truly Christian manner while reminding us that our lives are God's gift to us.

The second mistaken idea is that the only thing that God wants from us is unthinking obedience. You can be a good manager only if you think. What God wants of us is that we think about how we can best manage what He has entrusted to us.

This means that God wants us to become reflective, self-aware adults. God wants us to use our imaginations to explore ways to manage what God has entrusted to us. God wants us to think critically about how we have been doing things, with a view to finding better ways to do them. God expects us to plan carefully how we are to live our lives. God calls us to assess honestly whether our ways of managing things are effective.

Like the steward in Jesus' parable (Luke 16:1–13), we need to be shrewd about life. By making us stewards, God has in effect said this to us: *I am giving you your life and all these other gifts; now, you go and show Me what you can do with them.*

Needless to say, this is a little frightening. God says that we are responsible for what we do with our lives. It is therefore understandable that Christ followers sometimes try to evade this intimidating responsibility. The way we usually do this is by affirming our dependence upon God.

DEPENDENCE AND INDEPENDENCE

The image of steward affects our understanding of our dependence on God. There is a sense in which stewards are dependent on their owners for everything, because all that they have is what their owners have entrusted to them. But now that God has entrusted so much to us, our work is cut out for us, and we must do it, and do it wisely. We should not use our dependence on God as an excuse for not doing it. Dependence upon our master cannot be a substitute for managing what the master has entrusted to us.

One way to understand this is to recognize that dependence may take healthy or unhealthy forms. We can see this, for example, in the lives of children. It is healthy for children to depend on their parents to love them and to guide them wisely and sometimes to step in and help them out when they're unable to do things. But it is unhealthy for children to depend on their parents to do everything for them, or to refuse to grow up and accept responsibility, or to deny that they are responsible for the way they live their lives.

What God wants from us as stewards is dependence of the healthy kind. We are to trust that God has given our lives to us for a purpose, and that God loves us, and that God will sometimes help us with things that are beyond our powers. But we are not to use our trust in God as an excuse for refusing to grow up and accept the responsibility for what we do with our lives. One writer put it this way: "I can hear the objections. 'We are always infants in the arms of God.' Maybe. But God also wants us to be responsible, to grow up, to move toward being perfect even as God is perfect."[2]

Growing up is frightening; there is something comforting about remaining a child, depending on others to take care of all your needs, and having no responsibilities. But God does not want us to remain infants; God wants us to grow up. Seeing ourselves as stewards helps us to do that.

WHAT GOD HAS ENTRUSTED TO US

God has entrusted to us our lives and all we have. We can unpack what that means by reflecting briefly on some of the particular gifts God has given us.

Let us begin with our families. Our families of origin are God's gifts, and so are the families we create by marrying and by bringing children into the world. Our parents, our spouses, and our children are entrusted to us by God. God wants us to think carefully about our relationships with them all, and God wants us to make good decisions about how to make those relationships as Christian as they can possibly be. In managing our family relationships wisely, we are serving the God who owns them all and who entrusted them to us.

Managing family relationships is challenging. Beginning in early adulthood, we face so many questions. Whom should I marry, and when? How many children should we have, and when? How do I resolve family conflicts? How do I make my marriage flourish? How do I relate to aging and ill parents? How do I handle my failures? What do I do when a family member lets me down or betrays me? There are many such questions, and God calls us, as stewards of our families, to think about them wisely and shrewdly and to act in a timely manner to manage them well, for the sake of the God who owns it all.

Then there is the matter of our work, our careers, and our vocations. Like our families, these are God's gifts to us, and God calls us to manage them wisely. And as we all know, that can be very challenging. What sort of education or training do I need for my work? How do I get it, and how do I pay for it? Which position ought I to accept? How do I combine my ambition to succeed with my Christian concern that others also succeed? How much of my limited time, attention, and energy do I devote to my work, and how much to my family? How do I manage the money I earn? How do I use my office or position for the benefit of the church?

Then there is the matter of knowledge. Over the years of our lives each of us learns things, and this raises questions. What do I attempt to learn? How do I share what I have learned with others? How do I pass along a tradition of learning to a younger generation of Christians?

Then there is the matter of spiritual gifts. Spiritual gifts are forms of empowerment that God gives to Christians so that they will be able to carry out the work that God wants them to do. Paul taught that God gives one or more spiritual gifts to every Christian (1 Corinthians 12:6–7). Naturally we must be good stewards of these gifts, and that can be challenging. How do I know what my gifts are? How do I develop my gifts? How do I put my gifts to the most productive possible use? What should my attitude be as I attempt to use my gifts? How do I manage all this?

Peter gave specific instructions about two of the gifts (see 1 Peter 4:11), namely, speech and service. Those who have the gift of speaking must speak just as if their words were God's own words; in other words, they should speak the truth, in love, of the gospel of Jesus, and do it humbly rather than proudly (see Ephesians 4:15, Romans 1:16, 1 Peter 3:15–16). Those who have the gift of service to others should use all the energy God gives them to help others; they should not be lazy, and they should not waste their energy. For them, there is always the difficult question of balancing their care for the needs of others with caring for their own needs.

Then there is the matter of money. While it is unfortunate

that we in the church have sometimes restricted our stewardship to one of money and thereby overlooked that we are stewards of many things other than money, it is true that money is something God has entrusted to us. Like the earlier topics, stewardship of money generates numerous questions. How much of my time and energy do I give to earning money? What sacrifices should I be willing to make to earn more money, and what sacrifices ought I not be willing to make just to earn more? How do I manage what I earn? How much of my money should I give away, and through what organizations or to what individuals should I give it? How much control should I attempt to exert over how my gifts of money are used? Should I give to every poor person I happen to meet, or to some selected persons, or to none? How much money should I invest for the future of my family and myself, and how should I invest it?

One of the wisest sermons I ever read on this topic was preached by John Wesley and published in 1760. Pointing out how frequently non-Christians talk about money and how rarely Christians talk about it, Wesley called his listeners and readers to learn "the right use of money." His sermon had three points. First, "gain all you can"—use your common-sense and work hard at honorable tasks which do not harm you or others. Second, "save all you can"—don't waste your energies or talents or earnings, and don't indulge in frivolous things. Third, "give all you can"—always remember that God owns it all and that you are the steward rather than the owner of your wealth.[3] I think John Wesley had a very Christian understanding of the stewardship of money.

It is not difficult to see that, if we are to be good managers of our families, our work, our knowledge, our spiritual gifts, and our money, we are going to have to be both thoughtful and conscientious. Christians are always being encouraged to be conscientious; perhaps it would be well if we were encouraged more often to be thoughtful as well. Naturally, we may hope that our church will assist us to grow into thoughtful, conscientious stewards.

THE CHURCH'S STEWARDSHIP

We have seen that Paul told the Corinthians to think of church leaders "as servants of Christ and stewards of God's mysteries" (1 Corinthians 4:1). The church's leaders are managers of the gospel of the Lord. Since we do not often think in these terms, let us take a moment to reflect on it.

We may begin by considering who the leaders of the church are. Paul was thinking about himself and other apostles and preachers. There are still churches today in which ordained clergy play roles similar to those of the first apostles; in those churches the clergy are the principal stewards of God's mysteries.

However, many Christians today are members of churches in which the responsibility for decision-making for the church is shared by all its members; these churches seek the Lord's will by praying and talking together in order to arrive at a consensus about what the church should do. In these churches, all members are responsible for the management of the gospel that God has entrusted to them.

We can't think about this responsibility helpfully until we first recognize two natural assumptions. One is the assumption that there are already people in the church who know exactly how to manage the gospel, and the other is the assumption is that all Christians naturally, without even thinking about it, know how to manage the gospel. Neither of these assumptions is true. No one knows all there is to know about the best way to manage the gospel in our world today, and none of us naturally knows how to manage it. Once we have seen that these assumptions are untrue, we can begin to take seriously our responsibilities as stewards of God's mysteries.

In the past the church has managed the gospel in many ways, and perhaps most of them should be continued. Here are four examples: We have sent lifetime missionaries to preach the gospel to people who have not heard it, we have printed and distributed gospel tracts, we have purchased time to broadcast church worship services on radio and television, and we have established Christian colleges.

Stewards need to ask this question: are these wise and effective ways to manage the gospel, or are there better ways to do so? I think a case can be made for each of these ways, but I also recognize that each one can be questioned.

For example, should all missionaries serve for a lifetime, or should some plan to serve for a limited time only? Should we put the gospel, which is the most profound and important message in the world, into little tracts, which seem by their length and format to suggest that their content is superficial? Is it right to broadcast worship services, when surely what is needed is for people to be participants in the worship of God rather than observers of it? In view of the fact that colleges are institutions of higher education rather than of Christian community, is it not misleading to attempt to teach the gospel in them?

The point of all this is simply that, since we are stewards of the mysteries of God, we should give attention to what to do with the gospel.

I do not say this idly. I myself think the church today is facing some important questions about its stewardship of the mysteries of God. Here are some of the ones that seem most urgent to me. Is it right for our missionaries to go into countries under false pretenses? Is it right to spend missions money to support expensive institutions such as hospitals and schools? Is it right for worship services to be designed not to help Christians worship God but to attract non-Christians? Is it right for us to include in our worship services whatever styles of music happen to be popular in our culture? Is it right for congregations to spend most or even all of their money on themselves and their local ministries? Is it right for denominations to separate themselves so carefully from other denominations?

The point of all this is, of course, that we must be good managers of the gospel that God has entrusted to us. Paul shouldered the responsibility for the gospel in his time, and we know how he responded; we must shoulder the responsibility for the very same gospel in our very different time. (Incidentally, I think the answer to some of the questions above is yes and to others, no.)

CONCLUSION

One of my favorite hymns is by the American Quaker poet, John Greenleaf Whittier. It is entitled "Dear Lord and Father of Mankind," and one of the verses contains this prayer:

Drop Thy still dews of quietness,
Till all our strivings cease;
Take from our souls the strain and stress,
And let our ordered lives confess
The beauty of Thy peace.[4]

I love Whittier's phrase "our ordered lives," and I believe that, to the extent that our lives are ordered Christianly, to that extent we shall have been good stewards of the lives God has given to us.

CHAPTER 4

*"Fight the good fight
of the faith."*

—1 Timothy 6:12

Soldier

In the last chapter we noticed that almost no one in America today is routinely described as a steward. The opposite is true of soldiers; there are hundreds of thousands of soldiers in our nation today.

This is an interesting time for Americans to think about Christians as soldiers. Apparently America is the first nation in human history to exercise global military dominance. During the time when I was writing this book, the United States was engaged in a war against terrorists and a war against insurgents in Iraq. Whatever else may be said about the image of Christians as soldiers, it cannot be said that the image is unfamiliar to us.

The image was familiar in the era of the New Testament as well. Roman soldiers were stationed throughout the Mediterranean world, and Rome's military dominance was as well known then as America's is today.

Jesus encountered Roman soldiers on several different occasions. For example, He healed a Roman officer's servant (Matthew 8:5–13). And, of course, it was Roman soldiers who crucified Jesus.

The early Christians also routinely encountered Roman soldiers, so it must have been meaningful to the first readers of the New Testament documents, as it is to ourselves, to reflect upon the ways in which our Christian self-understanding is enriched by thinking of ourselves as soldiers.

The writer who made the greatest use of the image of soldier was Paul. He spoke of two of his colleagues, Epaphroditus and Archippus, as fellow soldiers (Philippians 2:25, Philemon 2). He urged the young pastor Timothy to "fight the good fight of the faith" (1 Timothy 6:12). Near the end of his own life he said, "I have fought the good fight" (2 Timothy 4:7). On several occasions he spoke about the need for things such as "the armor of light" (Romans 13:12) and "weapons of righteousness for the right hand and for the left" (2 Corinthians 6:7). In his very first letter he told the church at Thessalonica, "Put on the breastplate of faith and love, and for a helmet the hope of salvation" (1 Thessalonians 5:8). He wrote a long description of Christian armor to the church at Ephesus (Ephesians 6:10–17).

CHRISTUS VICTOR

The early Christians believed that Jesus Himself had engaged in a battle against demonic powers and that at His cross He had won a victory over them. In the desert He resisted the devil's three temptations (Matthew 4:1–11), and during His public ministry He performed exorcisms, casting demons out of people's lives (Mark 5:1–20). Even His death on the cross was a blow against the demons: "He disarmed the rulers and authorities [the cosmic, demonic forces at work in political enterprises] and made a public example of them, triumphing over them in [the cross]" (Colossians 2:15). The author of Hebrews said that Jesus shared our human condition "so that through death he might destroy the one who has the power of death, that is, the devil, and free those who all their lives were held in slavery by the fear of death" (Hebrews 2:14–15).

The early Christians believed that, since Christ had won a decisive victory over all evil forces on Good Friday and Easter, it was certain that the soldiers in His army would themselves be victorious: "In all these things we are more than conquerors" (Romans 8:37). John said that Christians would experience victory: "Whatever is born of God conquers the world. And this is the victory that conquers the world, our faith" (1 John 5:4).

However, this confidence that Christian soldiers would finally be victorious did not mean that they would not have to struggle and to suffer. After all, struggle and suffering are part of the life of a soldier: "Share in suffering like a good soldier of Christ Jesus" (2 Timothy 2:3). It is through struggle and suffering that Christian victories are won.

VIOLENCE AND CHRISTIAN FAITH

Before we explore what it means to us to be Christ's soldiers, we will consider a problem related to this image. The problem is that soldiers carry out violent activities; they destroy property, and they injure and kill people. How can military violence be an appropriate way to think about the lives of those who are trying to follow "the Prince of Peace" (Isaiah 9:6)? At Jesus' birth the angels announced the coming of peace on earth (Luke 2:14), and Jesus said quite clearly, "Blessed are the peacemakers, for they will be called children of God" (Matthew 5:9). How can followers of the Prince of Peace be soldiers?

The earliest Christians did not think they could. Here is how Roland Bainton, one of our great historians, expressed it:

The age of persecution down to the time of Constantine was the age of pacifism to the degree that during this period no Christian author to our knowledge approved of Christian participation in battle.... From the end of the New Testament period to the decade a.d. 170–180 there is no evidence whatever of Christians in the army.[1]

Today, of course, some churches are still committed to pacifism; the most famous peace churches are the Amish, the Brethren, the Mennonites, and the Quakers. Moreover, some Christians in a variety of churches today want to discontinue the use of militaristic imagery for Christian life: "Many have rejected the concept of warfare as a metaphor for the Christian endeavor because of a conviction that it fosters violent attitudes," states Harriet Crabtree.[2] Some have, for example, published hymnals in which no references to Christian warfare appear. This is certainly understandable. None of us wants to contribute anything to increasing the violence that is so widespread in our world.

But there are two problems with discarding the image of soldier for Christians. One is that you deprive yourself of a biblical teaching, and the other is that you overlook an important truth about our Christian lives; that truth, which becomes self-evident once you think about it, is that Christian life does, in fact, involve conflict, and it is unrealistic to think otherwise.

So if we are to be biblical and also to be realistic about life, we need to recognize that we are soldiers in Christ's army. But if we think of ourselves as soldiers, how can we avoid contributing to the awful conflict and violence of our world? It helps, I think, to recognize the nature of the enemies we face in our Christian war. There are, it seems to me, three classes of enemies.

First, there are cosmic enemies. These are the "rulers and authorities" about which Paul spoke when he said that

Christ had disarmed them and triumphed over them by His cross (Colossians 2:15).

Second, there are human beings who are opposed to Christian faith and to Christian moral values. There are many such people in our world today.

Third and finally, there are the enemies within each of us. It was of these that James spoke of when he wrote:

No one, when tempted, should say, "I am being tempted by God"; for God cannot be tempted by evil and he himself tempts no one. But one is tempted by one's own desire, being lured and enticed by it; then, when that desire has conceived, it gives birth to sin, and that sin, when it is fully grown, gives birth to death. Do not be deceived, my beloved.

—James 1:13–16

Those conflicts and disputes among you, where do they come from? Do they not come from your cravings that are at war within you? You want something and do not have it; so you commit murder.

—James 4:1–2

In summary, the enemies of the Christian soldier are cosmic powers, human beings, and our own inner impulses, and it is against them that we fight.

Or do we? I think that we as Christians are called to fight against the first and third groups. But what about the second group, the human beings who resist the gospel and

94

who reject Christian moral values—are we called to fight them?

I do not think so, and the reason is that in the New Testament Paul taught explicitly that we are not to fight against human beings. In the longest passage about Christians as soldiers that we have (Ephesians 6:10–17), Paul said emphatically and clearly:

Our struggle is not against enemies of blood and flesh, but against the rulers, against the authorities, against the cosmic powers of this present darkness, against the spiritual forces of evil in the heavenly places.

—Ephesians 6:12

I believe this: "Our struggle is not against enemies of blood and flesh." We are not called to fight against people. This seems very important to me. Christians are called by Christ to be soldiers and to engage in a continuing battle against spiritual forces, but, as in their relations with their fellow human beings, they are called not to fight but to "proclaim the gospel of peace" (Ephesians 6:15), which presumably includes that they "live peaceably with all" (Romans 12:18) and work as peacemakers (Matthew 5:9).

In summary, Christians are soldiers who live peaceably with all people but who fight fiercely against external and internal spiritual forces.

That is, of course, consistent with Jesus' life. He did no violence to His human opponents; it was they who

95

crucified Him, not the other way around. Paradoxically, it was in His (apparent) defeat by His human enemies on Good Friday that He won His decisive victory over the spiritual "rulers and authorities" (Colossians 2:15).

But is this realistic? Can we really fight effectively against spiritual forces without fighting against the people who are their agents (and victims too, of course) in the world? Can we, for example, fight against pornography without fighting pornographers? Can we fight sin without fighting sinners? I believe we can. I know that at times it may be difficult to know exactly how to do it, but I think we must try.

One necessary step is to have the courage and honesty to acknowledge that many of the spiritual forces we encounter are internal rather than external. The problem isn't in those other people out there, so much as it is in me. The cartoonist Walt Kelly created a character named Pogo who famously said on one occasion, "We have met the enemy, and it is us." His grammar may not have been correct, but his insight is consistent with James's teaching that our spiritual battles are against internal enemies.

In fact, it seems to me that Paul was thinking about internal enemies throughout much of the long passage about armor (Ephesians 6:10–17). The soldier is to wear the belt of truth; that means we must tell the truth, not lie or dissemble; the struggle to be truthful is a struggle against the inner temptation to be untruthful. The soldier is to put on the breastplate of righteousness; that means be a person who is good and holy and pure, not an unholy person; the struggle to be righteous is an internal struggle.

It takes maturity to admit that I myself am often my most threatening spiritual enemy. It is immature to assume that others are always the problem and that I am not. Our struggle against the spiritual powers is usually an internal struggle.

No one had a firmer grasp on this truth than the desert mothers and fathers. At about the beginning of the fourth century devout Christian men and women left the comforts of Hellenistic civilization for the deserts of Egypt and Syria, there to fight against the spiritual powers that tempted them to live less than faithful Christian lives. One of them was named Sarah, and her story is representative:

They said of the Abbess Sarah that for thirteen years she was fiercely attacked by the demon of lust. And she never prayed that the battle should be stayed. But she used to say only this: "Lord, grant me strength."

They also said of her that the same demon of lust was once attacking her menacingly, and tempting her with vain thought of the world. But she kept fearing God in her soul and maintained the rigour of her fasting. And once when she climbed up on the roof to pray, the spirit of lust appeared to her in a bodily form and said to her: "You have beaten me, Sarah." But she replied: "It is not I who have beaten you, but my Lord the Christ."[3]

The desert mothers and fathers were sometimes eccentric,

but their serious struggles with their inner demons can serve as an example for us today. We too must struggle against "the desires of the flesh that wage war against the soul" (1 Peter 2:11) if we are to become good and faithful Christians.

We struggle against a variety of spiritual forces. We may have tendencies toward selfishness and narcissism to defeat. We may have addictions to overcome. We may have impulses to subdue, and emotions to understand and to manage. We may have violence to restrain. We are engaged in moral and spiritual struggles against a wide range of enemies.

THE RESOURCES OF SOLDIERS

What resources do Christian soldiers have for their struggles?

One of our resources is "the word of God" which is "sharper than any two-edged sword" and is "able to judge the thoughts and intentions of the heart" (Hebrews 4:12). The writer may have been thinking about the Word of God as preached and taught in the church rather than as written down (since the books of the New Testament had not yet been written and collected together); in any case, we today understand that the Bible—not merely as an object of paper and ink but as a message of truth and life—is an indispensable resource for us. If we will study it closely and take it seriously, it can help us understand the thoughts and intentions of our own hearts and thereby to live as more faithful Christians.

A second resource is the subject of the Bible, namely, "the love of God in Christ Jesus our Lord" which makes it possible for us to be "more than conquerors" (Romans 8:39, 37). God's love is a strong, reassuring, comforting, helping love; as we live with confidence that God loves us and is helping us, we are empowered for our spiritual struggles.

A third resource is our trust that God loves us and helps us in our lives. "This is the victory that conquers the world, our faith" (1 John 5:4).

Trust in the love of God revealed in the Bible—those are certainly resources for our struggle to be good Christians. To those we might add the help provided to us in our fight by the rest of God's huge army—the entire Christian church—with its fellowship, its worship services, its ordinances of baptism and the Lord's Supper, and its many and varied ministries. We can depend on the fact that God has provided us with the resources necessary for us to be good soldiers. "The weapons of our warfare are not merely human, but they have divine power" (2 Corinthians 10:4).

SOLDIERS ARE LOYAL

What are our responsibilities as soldiers?

Our first responsibility is loyalty. We must be unconditionally loyal to "the enlisting officer" (2 Timothy 2:4) who recruited us, Jesus Christ. Apparently it was characteristic of the armies that served Rome that they were created, not directly by the government, but by wealthy individuals who brought them together, armed and trained them, and then put them at the disposal of Rome. Naturally the result of this arrangement was that Roman soldiers had an absolute commitment to the individual who enlisted them, the enlisting officer of 2 Timothy 2:4.

One of the things that characterizes the Christian faith is that it is a commitment, not simply to a creed or a code of conduct or a set form of worship, but to a Person, Jesus Christ. Our loyalty is not just to a way of life, but to our enlisting and commanding officer.

In addition, we must be unconditionally loyal to our fellow soldiers. It is an act of treason to fail to support your comrades-in-arms, and in armies even today it is punishable by death. In my judgment we in the army of the Lord need to hear this afresh today. Instead of disagreeing with and arguing against and criticizing our fellow-soldiers, we need to support them by prayer and friendship. We are, after all, in the same army here, not in opposing armies.

SOLDIERS MUST PREPARE
AND SUFFER

Our second responsibility as soldiers is to train and to prepare for our struggles. Soldiers are made, not born, and we must learn how to fight the battles that our commanding officer calls us to fight. That involves study and thoughtfulness and being observant. We must not suppose that we already know all that is necessary in order to "fight the good fight of the faith" (1 Timothy 6:12).

A third responsibility concerns the hardships of spiritual soldiery. Military training isn't easy, and neither is fighting once the battles are under way. We must be prepared to "share in suffering like a good soldier of Christ Jesus" (2 Timothy 2:3). As Christians, we do not believe that the world is a hedonistic paradise designed to make us all just as happy as possible. It is a fallen world; it's not the way it was created to be. Christ suffered and struggled in our world, and so will those of us who serve in His army. There are times of intense joy in life, of course, but there also are times of suffering, sometimes great suffering, and a well-informed Christian will not be caught off-guard when a time for suffering comes. Anyone who argues that, since Christians are "more than conquerors," they will always be healthy and successful and prosperous simply hasn't been attentive to the full message of the New Testament.

So our third responsibility, after loyalty to our commanding officer and our fellow soldiers and training and preparation, is to endure whatever sufferings may come our way. We have the pattern of Christ to guide us in this endurance: "Christ also suffered for you, leaving you an example, so that you should follow in his steps" (1 Peter 2:21). We are to endure our sufferings the way Christ endured His.

So we ask, how did Christ endure His sufferings? He

always understood that part of His life's work was to make sacrifices on behalf of others, to serve rather than to be served (see Matthew 20:28). He did not seek out needless suffering (see John 10:17–18); in fact, He sought to avoid suffering where possible (see Matthew 26:39). When He could not avoid suffering, He accepted it without surprise or complaint. He did not retaliate against those who caused His suffering, but instead He forgave them (Luke 23:34). He learned from His sufferings (see Hebrews 5:8).

Christian soldiers must follow the example of their commanding officer. We must accept Jesus' paradoxical teaching that the point of our lives is not to be served but to serve, and we must recognize that sometimes that will involve sacrifice on our part. We should not seek out point-less suffering, and we are certainly free to avoid suffering where that is possible. When we can't avoid it, we are not to be surprised by it or to complain about it. We are not to hit back against those who cause us suffering but rather forgive them. And we ought to learn from our suffering.

SOLDIERS MUST FIGHT THE GOOD FIGHT OF FAITH

Our fourth and final responsibility is simply to "fight the good fight" (1 Timothy 6:12). There wouldn't be much point in our being loyal and training and preparing and enduring suffering if we did not go on to actually engage in battle. As we have seen, our battle is not against human beings, but against the spiritual powers that are most likely to be found in our own hearts. We are to use the resources at our disposal to try to overcome our dark impulses.

CONCLUSION

Christians may and should live at peace with human beings, but we cannot and should not attempt to live at peace with the dark spiritual powers that are the enemies of our souls. With spiritual determination but without physical violence, we should fight moral and spiritual battles in order to achieve "a good conscience" (1 Timothy 1:19) and "to please the enlisting officer," Jesus Christ (2 Timothy 2:4).

CHAPTER 5

"I have finished the race."

—2 Timothy 4:8

Athlete

A s I am writing this book, the world's attention is once again focused on the Olympic Games. This year they are being held in Greece, their original home, and athletes from more than 200 nations are competing.

In the ancient world many nations valued athletics highly, but the nation of Israel was not one of them. There is a revealing story about this in the book of Second Maccabees, a book that is found in Catholic Bibles but not in most Protestant Bibles. The story is about a vicious pagan, Antiochus Epiphanes, who ruled Israel in the second century before Christ. Antiochus attempted to introduce paganism into the life of Israel and to eradicate Israel's faith in the Lord. One of his strategies in this evil task was to allow one of his officers to "set up a gymnasium for the physical education of young men" so that young Jews would "conform to the Greek way of life." The effort was partially successful, so that "the priests no longer showed any enthusiasm for their duties at the altar" of the Lord, preferring instead to "join in the sports at the wrestling school in defiance of the law" (2 Maccabees 4:7–17 REB).

Given this history, it is understandable that many Jews came to associate competitive sports with paganism. The original Olympics themselves were held in honor of the Greek god Zeus.

This means that much of what the writers of the New Testament knew about athletics came to them from their knowledge of the Hellenistic and Roman worlds in which they lived at least part of their lives. The Greek language, in which of course the New Testament was written, included several words related to athletics. For example, the Greek word *athleo*, from which we get the English word *athlete*, meant "I compete" (it appears in 2 Timothy 2:5); the Greek word *gumnasia*, from which we get the English word *gymnasium*, meant "discipline" (see 1 Timothy 4:7–8); and the Greek word *stadion*, from which comes our English word *stadium*, meant "a race" (see 1 Corinthians 9:24).

In the New Testament the athletic event mentioned most frequently is a race; this seems usually to have been a race by an individual, but sometimes it may refer to a relay race run by several persons (see, for example, Hebrews 12:1). Boxing is also mentioned (see 1 Corinthians 9:24–27).

Life, the writers of the New Testament were telling us, is like a race (or a boxing match), and there is a lot to be learned from this fact. In order to compete successfully we must train (1 Timothy 4:7–10), and we must be self-disciplined (1 Corinthians 9:27). We must run hard (Philippians 2:16), and we must carefully follow the rules of the game (2 Timothy 2:5). We must be prepared to suffer in order to run well (Hebrews 12:1–2). As we run we are being watched by great crowds of people (Hebrews 12:1–2). It is not enough to run part of the race; we must persevere to the end (Hebrews 12:1–2). We must always keep our eyes on Jesus, who runs ahead of us (Hebrews 12:1–2) and who has determined what course each of us is to run (Acts 20:24). We run so that the Lord, who is the judge (2 Timothy 4:7–8), will award us the prize which is an imperishable crown of life and glory (1 Corinthians 9:24–27, Revelation 2:10, 1 Peter 5:4).

COMPETITION AND LOVE

As a rule, races are competitive. In a race, there are winners and there are losers. The goal is to be a winner, and that means that the goal is that others will be losers.

But when we think about our lives as Christians, we realize that we do not want to act in ways that cause others to be losers. As Christians, we want everyone to succeed and no one to fail. How can we do this if we are athletes?

We have a way around this problem today, and that is to think about what athletes call personal best. This phrase refers to the fact that I run, for example, the 100-meter race at the fastest speed I've ever run it. This is done without reference to the speed at which anyone else does it. There is no competition here, except against myself. It is not necessary for others to fail in order for me to succeed.

Several passages in the New Testament suggest that the race we Christians are running is not competitive. For example, Paul wrote to Timothy, "I have finished the race, I have kept the faith. From now on there is reserved for me the crown of righteousness, which the Lord, the righteous judge, will give me on that day, and not only to me but also to all who have longed for his appearing" (2 Timothy 4:7–8). Certainly Peter was not concerned that he would lose a competition when he told his readers, "You will win the crown of glory that never fades away" (1 Peter 5:4).

Recently a French scholar argued that this concept was well known in the ancient world: "One might think that the image of life as a race is intended to highlight speed or winning; in fact…the metaphor was more generally employed to indicate the idea of steady progress."[1]

So we want to run our race well, and we also want others to run their races well.

What is the proper place for competition in the life of a Christian? We see competition in so many aspects of modern life. Is competition a good thing, or a bad one?

In my judgment, there are sectors of our lives where competition helps us, and there are sectors where it hurts us.

Obviously, competition helps in athletics; as we compete with others, we achieve more than we otherwise might, and so do the others. Competition also helps in economics; as we compete to earn more, we are helped to create better products and services than we otherwise might. Doubtless there are other areas in which competition is helpful.

But there also are areas of life in which competition is disastrous. It is disastrous, for example, for a wife and husband to compete with each other, or for parents to put their children in competition with each other (children have a natural tendency to compete with each other). It is impossible to have strong marriages or families if competition invades our homes in these ways. Competition is destructive of friendships and of other relationships that involve love and trust and understanding.

In his book *Connect*, psychiatrist Edward M. Hallowell wrote the following: "For most people, the two most important experiences in life are achieving and connecting. Almost everything that counts is directed toward one of these two goals. The peaks of life for most people are falling in love (connecting) and reaching a hard-won goal (achieving)."[2] I find the distinction between achieving and connecting very insightful, and it seems to me that as a general rule competition is sometimes appropriate when our goal is achieving but never appropriate when our goal is connecting.

For Christians, the principal concern in life is connecting, for Jesus taught us that the meaning of our lives is to love God with all our hearts and to love our neighbors as ourselves (Matthew 22:34–40). But achieving is important for us too; some of the biblical images for Christians emphasize connecting (friends, children), and others emphasize achieving (soldier, steward, athlete). When we are using the images that emphasize achieving, we need to remind ourselves that our ultimate goal is connecting with—loving—God and our neighbors.

Some thoughtful observers today believe that even in competitive athletics in the literal sense, it is possible to incorporate the altruistic notion that we do not want others to fail. At a conference at St. Olaf College in Minnesota in June 2004, the college pastor Bruce Benson suggested that there is a difference between sport and athletics. Sport, he said, is whether you win or lose; athletics is how you play the game. Sport is about glamour; athletics is about beauty. Sport creates stars and crowds and mobs; athletics creates teammates and community.[3]

With these distinctions in mind, citizens in societies in which athletics plays such a commanding role may be helped to understand their lives as Christians by thinking of themselves as athletes.

CHRIST AND THE CHURCH

If Christ followers are all athletes, then how are we to think of Christ, and of the church?

In the New Testament Christ is spoken of as the one who has set us an example of how to run the race (Hebrews 12:1–2) and also as the judge who decides what our reward will be (Revelation 2:10). To these images we today might add that Christ is the trainer or coach who helps us to become the best athletes we can be. The image of Christ as coach has proven to be of enormous help to many Christians who have engaged in competitive sports and who have been helped and influenced by dedicated coaches. All of us understand the testimony of the Christian athlete who says, "I've played on several teams with different coaches, but now I'm playing on the best team with the best Coach there is."

The church is, of course, the Christian team. In a time when the church is divided along almost every conceivable line, appreciating all Christians as our fellow teammates is one of the most urgent duties of Christians today.

TRAINING

Most of us today understand, at least in principal, that great athletes are able to do what they do in large measure because they have trained to do it. We usually don't see the training; what we see is what the training makes possible. But we know the training is important.

And it is important for Christians, also; we cannot run

our race without seriously training.

But what is Christian training? When does it happen, and where do we find it? In connection with the image of disciple, we have already reviewed our need to learn about Christian living; in connection with the image of steward we have reviewed our need to think shrewdly about how to manage our lives; we spoke about training also in connection with the image of soldier. Is there anything else to say about training?

Yes, there is, and it is spoken of in several of the New Testament passages to which we have alluded. For example, "athletes exercise self-control" (1 Corinthians 9:25), "train yourselves" (1 Timothy 4:7), and "lay aside every weight" (Hebrews 12:1). These passages speak about the sacrifice and self-discipline of athletes. Athletes do not simply learn the facts about how to run swiftly; they discipline themselves sacrificially so that they will be able to run swiftly.

Christians are to do the same. Part of our training is to decide about appropriate forms of sacrificial self-discipline that will help us to run our Christian race well.

It is important for us to remember that there are forms of self-discipline that are not appropriate for us. In some of his letters the apostle Paul warned against inappropriate forms of discipline. For example, "Do not let anyone condemn you in matters of food and drink or of observing festivals, new moons, or sabbaths....Do not let anyone disqualify you, insisting on self-abasement" (Colossians

2:16, 18). Apparently some leaders had urged the Christians in Colosse to undergo inappropriate forms of self-discipline, and Paul vigorously opposed that.

So what is appropriate sacrificial self-discipline? Probably there is no one answer to this question that fits all Christians at all times in their lives, but we can consider some of the forms of self-discipline that have been widely accepted by Christians across the centuries.

I will mention just three: prayer, meditation, and contemplation. Prayer is talking to God, who loves us and who therefore listens to us and responds to us when we pray. Meditation is taking a phrase from Scripture, such as "I fear no evil" (Psalm 23:4) and quietly saying it over and over again, until it becomes a part of who we are. Contemplation is sitting in silence before God, not employing any words, either the words of Scripture or our own words, but quietly and intentionally being with God. These three disciplines all equip us to run the race better, and all of them are available to all Christ followers.

These three practices are forms of sacrifice. We give up some of our time and some other activities in order to carry them out.

But, you may say, how can you say that it is a sacrifice to spend time with the Lord? Of course, that might be asked of any sacrifice we attempt to make for the Lord. We always receive more than we give, no matter what the practice is.

About 1611 a child named Nicholas Hermann was born

in France. As a young man he fought in the Thirty Years War and was captured by enemy soldiers. He was scheduled to be executed as a spy, but because of a clerical error he was released instead. He went to Paris and entered a monastery, not as a monk but as a lay brother, working in the kitchen. He took the name Brother Lawrence, and he became famous for his life of prayer. He undertook what he called "the practice of the presence of God." Over the years he trained himself to be aware at every moment throughout the day that God was present with him, and to act accordingly. He said that our goal in life "did not depend upon changing [what we are doing], but in doing that for God's sake which we commonly do for our own." He found that even going into a monastery was not really a sacrifice: "He said that he went into the monastery in order to sacrifice, but that God had disappointed him, as he had met with nothing but satisfaction."[4]

Brother Lawrence was surely right; it is impossible, really, to sacrifice anything for God, because God has given us everything good that we have (James 1:17); we always receive more from God than we give to God. Still, there is a limited sense in which we can live lives of sacrificial self-discipline, by replacing selfish and self-indulgent practices with ones that equip us to run the race more swiftly. Prayer, meditation, and contemplation are all in that sense acts of sacrificial self-discipline.

RUNNING

It is difficult to imagine an athlete who trains rigorously but then never participates in a race, and certainly that is not the ideal for Christians, either. It is not enough to pray and meditate and contemplate; we also must engage in Christian living. Drawing upon the strength we have gained from our training, we run steadily the race that the Lord sets before us.

That means that, every day, we attempt to live as we know faithful Christians ought to live. We are careful to give as well as to take. We listen as well as speak. We speak truthfully and do not dissemble. We work hard and resist laziness. We are honest, not dishonest. We are patient and courageous. We keep our promises and our vows.

One of my former pastors, Dr. Luther Joe Thompson, sometimes said in his sermons, "For me, it is not so much a matter of knowing God's will as of doing it," and I think there is a great truth there. Christians who have read the Bible and gone to church for years may have a very full knowledge of the race God has set before them; while we may need sometimes to study the race, there is another sense in which the important thing is just to run it. And in the running, we will learn the things we need to know about it.

FINISHING

In a 100-meter race, nothing is gained if you are the world's fastest 40-meter runner but are unable to complete 100 meters. In our lives as Christians, nothing is gained if we make a start at living as a Christian but do not complete the race. Jesus says to us all, "Be faithful until death, and I will give you the crown of life" (Revelation 2:10).

Perhaps you personally know people who made a good start on the Christian race but who, for one reason or another, have not continued to run. They no longer participate in the life of the church, they no longer pray, and they no longer "press on toward the goal for the prize of the heavenly call of God in Christ Jesus" (Philippians 3:14). This is, of course, deeply regrettable, and it makes us sad, but it does happen.

People fail to complete the race for various reasons; here I want to consider just one. It is that their understanding of their faith did not grow along with the rest of their lives. They continue growing intellectually and emotionally and relationally and vocationally and so on, but they feel obliged to keep their understanding of their faith in the pre-adolescent or adolescent stage in which they first became aware of it.

People who are grown-up adults in other sectors of their lives but children in their faith are always tempted to assume that faith is a matter for children rather than for adults, and, when they do, to set faith aside. It is tragic that they have not seen that the problem is not that faith, which after all has been treasured by some of the wisest and best and most mature persons who ever lived on earth, is intrinsically adolescent; the problem is rather that they have refused to allow their faith to grow up. If we are to finish the race God has set before us, we will need to nurture rather than to stifle our growth in faith and hope and love.

REWARDS

In the New Testament there are frequent references to awards for those who finish their race, and the usual language for one's award is "crown" (see 1 Corinthians 9:24–27, 2 Timothy 2:5, 2 Timothy 4:7–8, 1 Peter 5:4, Revelation 2:10). In the ancient world a victorious athlete was given a crown in much the way modern athletes are given a trophy. A crown typically was made of small branches twisted together into a circle, sometimes with flowers intertwined with them.

What does it mean to say that following our deaths we will receive from the Lord a crown as the award for running our race well?

It certainly does not mean that we have lived in such a way as to earn our place in heaven; that is contrary to the New Testament message that says that it is by God's grace, and not by our good works (or by running the race well, either), that we are saved.

Still, we who have been saved by God's grace now have a "race that is set before us" by God (Hebrews 12:1). We will run that race well or poorly, and in the life to come God will reward us according to how well we have run it.

The entire idea of receiving a reward troubles many sincere Christians. They worry that, even if the idea of a

117

reward does not suggest that we somehow save ourselves by running well, serving the Lord for a reward suggests something mercenary, selfish, perhaps greedy, and certainly unworthy of Christians.

They have a point. It would be selfish and greedy to serve Christ with a mercenary spirit that said, *Well, this is the best investment I ever made, because it will pay me eternal dividends.* Christians should repudiate selfish motivations such as this.

If we repudiate selfish motivations, is there still a place for rewards? I think there is. I know of two popular ways to think of this. One is apparent in the following, very beautiful passage about the church's worship of God in heaven:

And whenever the living creatures give glory and honor and thanks to the one who is seated on the throne, who lives forever and ever, the twenty-four elders fall before the one who is seated on the throne and worship the one who lives forever and ever; they cast their crowns before the throne, singing, "You are worthy, our Lord and God, to receive glory and honor and power, for you created all things, and by your will they existed and were created."

—Revelation 4:9–11

The crowns are, as we saw above, the awards given to Christians who have run their race well. According to this passage, in heaven the elders do not clutch their crowns selfishly or greedily but rather offer them in worship to the God who conferred the crowns on them in the first place.

There is a similar idea about awards that is talked about in some church circles. It is that, in heaven, some Christians will have larger cups than others, that is, will have a larger capacity for receiving God's blessing, but all Christians will have their cups full of God's blessing. No one will be disappointed because everyone's cup will be filled, but the differences in the way we ran the race of life will be recognized.

The distinction between intrinsic and extrinsic awards comes into play here. Extrinsic awards are awards that have no necessary connection to our race; for example, a person who wins a certain race is given a large amount of money; there is no intrinsic connection between running and money. Intrinsic awards have necessary connections to our race; for example, a person who runs a certain race well has stamina for other races. Presumably, awards in heaven will be intrinsically connected to the race we ran on earth.

I want to make a confession here, because I think there is a chance that some readers of this book may have had the same experience I have. Across the years I have attempted to think of the Lord giving me rewards for the way I ran my race, but I have not been able to do it at a meaningful level. I simply have not been able to identify with the idea that I may receive a reward. I want to run my race well, and I want to run it to the end, and I want by the grace of God to be accepted by the Lord at the end, but I don't feel any passion for receiving a reward. To me it is enough to believe that in the end God will accept me and change me into a good person (see 1 John 3:2) and that I will live in a huge community of mutual love and trust and justice and peace and meaning with my fellow Christians and with God. Any reward beyond that just doesn't speak to me very deeply.

Perhaps this is just a way of saying that seeing the face of the Lord (see Revelation 22:4) will be its own reward. I don't know. But I thought I would mention this on the chance some of my readers may have similar feelings about rewards.

CONCLUSION

In a world in which athletes receive so much public attention and admiration, Christians may think of themselves as spiritual athletes who have been trained by Christ to run a race He has set for them and who, if they persevere to the end, are destined to receive a reward from Him for their faithfulness.

CHAPTER 6

> *"He looked forward to the city that has foundations."*
>
> —Spoken of Abraham in Hebrews 11:10

Traveler

The idea that Christians are travelers on a journey through life is widely accepted in the church today, and it should be, because, as we shall see in a moment, it is a biblical idea.

But the idea that life is like a journey did not originate with the Bible and is not peculiar to Christians. In many societies across many centuries there has been a sense that living through time is somehow like moving through space. Some of the world's great literature has been written on the assumption that life is a journey; this is true of Homer's *Odyssey* and

Virgil's *Aeneid*. In the Middle Ages, Chaucer's *Canterbury Tales* was about pilgrims telling each other stories as they traveled together to a sacred place. One of the most influential Christian devotional books is *The Pilgrim's Progress*, written by the Baptist pastor John Bunyan while he was in jail, a book that, according to Margaret Miles, "has informed all future use of the metaphor of Christian life as pilgrimage in the English-speaking world."[1] Here in the United States some of our well-known fiction is about journeys. Mark Twain's *Life on the Mississippi* is about a journey down our greatest river, and J. D. Salinger's *Catcher in the Rye* is about a young man, Holden Caulfield, wandering around in New York. A very funny and also very touching book is *Breakfast at Tiffany's* by Truman Capote; its central character has a business card with her name, Holiday Golightly, printed in the center; in the corner of the card where her business should be listed is a single word, "Traveling." She says that even though she doesn't know where she's going, she will know it when she gets there.

If we think of life as a journey, then our most urgent question is, is the journey a meaningless wandering, or does it have a meaningful destination? I find it interesting that our English words *destination* and *destiny* are so similar; if our life is a journey with a destination, then our lives have a destiny.

But do we? Or are we simply meandering with no ultimate destination? One of our fine Christian philosophers, Geddes MacGregor, thinks that, to the extent that you believe that your life has a destination, to that extent you are already a person of faith, however much or little that you may be aware of the fact: "Every pilgrim is somehow a Believer, in the sense that he has caught something, however vaguely, of the Believer's attitude and vision."[2] Unbelief, then, is to think that your life is not a pilgrimage with a meaningful destination, but rather a meaningless wandering through time and space; this is not an understanding that is naturally congenial to us as human beings.

Although the image of life as a journey is found outside the Bible, the Bible adds a great deal to our understanding of the journey of life.

JOURNEYS IN THE BIBLE

"The Bible is fundamentally a story of a people's journey with God."[3] In the Old Testament, emphasis is given to two journeys, one by an individual and the other by a nation. The individual was Abraham, who, together with his wife Sarah and their extended family and household, made the long journey from Ur, in modern Iraq, to the promised land of Canaan. The long journey of a nation was the Exodus of the people of Israel from slavery in Egypt through the wilderness to their new home in the promised land.

For Abraham and for the people of Israel, these were literal, geographical journeys. In the New Testament, each of these journeys is used as an image of the spiritual life of Christians. Abraham became a model of how Christians are to trust in God on their journeys: "By faith Abraham obeyed when he was called to set out for a place that he was to receive as an inheritance; and he set out, not knowing where he was going" (Hebrews 11:8). Similarly, the people of Israel at the Exodus are presented as an example of faith: "By faith the people passed through the Red Sea as if it were dry land" (Hebrews 11:29).

When we turn to the four Gospels, we are struck by the fact that Jesus was a traveler. He was an itinerant rabbi, and His disciples followed Him throughout Galilee, Samaria, and Judea, and occasionally outside the boundaries of Israel.

In theological terms Jesus' travels were much longer, for as the Son of God, He made a long journey from heaven to earth. Jesus taught this in His parable about an absentee landowner who sent his only son to the vineyard he owned (Mark 12:1–12), and Paul taught it when he spoke of Jesus as having descended from above and then re-ascended (Ephesians 4:8–9, Philippians 2:5–11). An assumption that Jesus journeyed to our world lies behind John's comment that "God did not send the Son into the world to condemn the world, but in order that the world might be saved through him" (John 3:17), and also behind Paul's observation that "though [Jesus] was rich, yet for your sakes he became poor" (2 Corinthians 8:9).

Since Abraham's life was a journey, and the people of Israel were delivered from slavery by making a journey, and Jesus' life was a journey, it certainly comes as no surprise to find that the writers of the New Testament treated the life of a Christian as a journey. Before we examine how they did this, we will give attention to one particular kind of journey that was more familiar in the world of the Bible than it is to many Christians today.

PILGRIMAGE

A pilgrimage is a journey made to a sacred place as an act of religious devotion. In the Old Testament era faithful Jews made pilgrimages to Jerusalem; as they walked up to the city (Jerusalem was built on four hills), they sang special psalms called *psalms of ascent*, some of which are recorded in the Book of Psalms (see, for examples, Psalms 24, 122, 125).

Mary and Joseph were making a pilgrimage when they took the then twelve-year-old Jesus to the Temple during the Passover festival (see Luke 2:41–51). As an adult Jesus continued the practice of pilgrimage, for at the end of His life He went as a pilgrim to Jerusalem during the Passover festival (Matthew 21:1–11).

Even after Paul had become a Christian, he continued to go occasionally on pilgrimage to Jerusalem (see Acts 20:16).

In the years immediately after the New Testament era, Christians tended not to go on pilgrimages to Jerusalem. Then, in the fourth century, the emperor Constantine and his successors made Christianity the official religion of the Roman Empire, and Christian pilgrimages to Jerusalem became popular: "the first famous pilgrim to Jerusalem was

Helena, mother of the emperor Constantine, who claimed to have discovered there a piece of the true cross. It was she who initiated popular interest in pilgrimage to the holy places."[4] Across the centuries many have followed her example, and today many Christians still go on pilgrimages, to Jerusalem or to some other sacred place. However, many others, especially Protestants, do not. How did it ever happen that some Christians do not go on pilgrimages?

One of the reasons is that many Christians have understood Jesus' teaching in John 4 to discourage the entire idea of pilgrimage. That passage records a conversation between Jesus and an unnamed woman at a well in Samaria; the well was named Jacob's Well, and it was located at the foot of Mount Gerizim, which was the holy mountain of the Samaritans just as Mount Zion (one of the hills on which Jerusalem was built) was the holy mountain of the Jews. During their conversation the woman asked Jesus whether it was more appropriate to worship God in Jerusalem, as the Jews do, or on Mount Gerizim, as the Samaritans do. Jesus replied, "The hour is coming when you will worship the Father neither on this mountain nor in Jerusalem....the true worshipers will worship the Father in spirit and truth" (John 4:21, 23). Many Christians have understood Jesus' words to mean that no place is holier than any other and that therefore it is possible to worship God wherever you are. If no place is holier than others, then, of course, a principal incentive for pilgrimages disappears.

On the other hand, in the very next chapter of his Gospel John records that Jesus went to Jerusalem for one of the Jewish festivals (John 5:1), which suggests that, whatever else Jesus may have meant while He was talking to the woman, He did not intend to put an end to all pilgrimages. And that leaves us with our present situation, in which many Christians continue to go on pilgrimages, to Jerusalem or other sacred places, and many others do not.

We have seen that the writers of the New Testament speak of a Christian's life as a journey. Did they ever speak of a Christian's life as a pilgrimage to a holy place?

In the King James Version of the Bible, the word *pilgrim* is used in the following two passages in the New Testament:

These all died in faith, not having received the promises, but having seen them afar off, and were persuaded of them, and embraced them, and confessed that they were strangers and pilgrims on the earth.

—Hebrews 11:13 KJV

Dearly beloved, I beseech you as strangers and pilgrims, abstain from fleshly lusts.

—1 Peter 2:11 KJV

In both of these passages the Greek word is *parepidemos*. This word appears in just one other passage, where it is translated *strangers*:

Peter, an apostle of Jesus Christ, to the strangers scattered throughout Pontus....

—1 Peter 1:1 KJV

In modern translations *parepidemos* is translated with a number of different English words including *foreigners, aliens, exiles,* and *refugees.* These words convey a sense that Christians are expatriates who are living far away from their real home. Another translation of *parepidemos* is *sojourners,* which combines the idea that a Christian is an expatriate with a suggestion that a Christian is a traveler whose life is a journey.

So much for the word itself. What about the image—does the New Testament present the idea that Christians are travelers and that they are on a journey to a sacred destination? Indeed it does, in the following passage, which the author intended to be both an appreciation of Abraham and a model of the life of Christians:

By faith Abraham obeyed when he was called to set out for a place that he was to receive as an inheritance; and he set out, not knowing where he was going.... he looked forward to the city that has foundations, whose architect and builder is God.... They confessed that they were strangers and foreigners on the earth, for people who speak in this way make it clear that they are seeking a homeland.... they desire a better country, that is, a heavenly one. Therefore God is not ashamed to be called their God; indeed, he has prepared a city for them.

—Hebrews 11:8–16

It seems to me that the author of this passage was calling Christians to think of their lives not only as journeys but also as pilgrimages toward a destination prepared by God. The church is therefore a community of pilgrims who are traveling toward a common destination.

What does this say to us about how we as Christians live our lives? We will reflect on three themes: We are not home yet, we are traveling, and it is certain that in the end we will arrive at home.

WE ARE NOT HOME YET

As Christians we believe two very different things about the world. On the one hand, it is God's good world, and we should love it as we love all the good things God has created. On the other hand, it is not the way it's supposed to be, and we should be wary of it. Creation and the Fall are both real.

We are so accustomed to both of these ideas that it is easy for us to overlook how sophisticated it is to hold both of them to be true. It is quite easy to hold either one alone. It's easy to believe that the world is good and is the way it's supposed to be; people who believe this risk becoming naïve, but their view is understandable. It's also easy to believe the world is fallen and evil; people who believe this risk becoming cynical, but their view is understandable.

It is much more difficult to hold both truths: this is God's good world, and it's also a fallen world. It is one of the success stories of the Jewish and Christian faiths that we have been taught to see both truths about the world. Even our children are able to grasp that both things are true.

Taken together, the two truths govern Christians' attitudes toward the world. On the one hand, Christians love this world. We know God made it; we know God loves it; we know Christ came into it to redeem it; we believe we belong in it; so we sing, "This is my Father's world." On the other hand, we distrust this world; we know it is fallen; we know it is a source of suffering to us, and a source of temptation; we believe we do not really belong in it, so we sing, "This world is not my home."

These two attitudes lead to two different kinds of behavior. On the one hand, we care for the world, and try to make it a better place. We give attention to it, and we work for its welfare. On the other hand, we "do not love the world or the things in the world" (1 John 2:15). We do not become needy for what the world gives, and we do not become "entangled in everyday affairs" of this world (2 Timothy 2:4).

The idea that we are expatriates like, for example, Americans who live for years in another country, is a perfect way to describe our relationship with the world. One of our important tasks as Christians is to learn how to be *in* the world without being *of* the world.

I think the best description I have ever read of how we are trying to relate to the world is found in a second-century document known as *The Epistle to Diognetus*. While we do not know very much about the historical context for this beautiful letter, we have no trouble understanding its message in the following passage:

Christians are not distinguished from the rest of humanity by country, language, or custom. For nowhere do they live in cities of their own, nor do they speak with some unusual dialect, nor do they practice an eccentric life-style.... While they live in both Greek and barbarian cities, as each one's lot was cast, and follow the local customs in dress and food and other aspects of life, at the same time they demonstrate the remarkable and admittedly unusual character of their own citizenship. They live in their own countries, but only as aliens; they participate in everything as citizens, and endure everything as foreigners.... They marry like everyone else, and have children, but they do not expose their offspring. They share their food but not their wives.... They live on earth, but their citizenship is in heaven.... In a word, what the soul is to the body, Christians are to the world. The soul is dispersed through all the members of the body, and Christians throughout the cities of the world. The soul dwells in the body, but is not of the body; likewise Christians dwell in the world, but are not of the world.... Such is the important position to which God has appointed them, and it is not right for them to decline it. [5]

Christians live in the world but not of it. They are here, really here, in the world, yet their citizenship lies elsewhere, in another world altogether. What a soul is to a body—really in it, but really different from it—so Christians are to the world.

Many parents who travel with small children have heard them ask, *Are we there yet?* The same question could be asked of all Christians: Are we there yet? And the answer for us is the same as for children: No, we're not there yet.

WE ARE TRAVELING

We could also say to our children that, even though we are not there yet, we are on the way. So it is with us as Christians; we are on the way.

What route are we taking? In a sense, the route is different for each of us. Each Christian has her own experiences and history and relationships and problems and solutions.

Still, across almost twenty centuries Christians who are aware of their journey have attempted to map out a general route for the journey that we all take. For example, John Bunyan did this in *Pilgrim's Progress*, and in our own time James Fowler has attempted to describe the *Stages of Faith*, as his book title suggests.

A map that I recently became interested in was proposed by Bernard of Clairvaux, a twelfth-century French monk and scholar. His book entitled *On the Love of God* is one of the most beautiful and influential of all the medieval books on the Christian journey. In it he proposed that the journey occurs in four stages, which he calls "the four degrees of love."[6]

In the first stage, we love ourselves for our own sake. This is natural for us, and it is where we all begin. According to Bernard, it is not sinful to love ourselves in this way, unless our love for ourselves leads us to refuse to love our neighbors.

We move to the second stage when we begin to love God for our own sake. While this love still has an element of selfishness in it, it is a genuine love for God, and so it represents an advance over the first stage. Bernard said that we should not be contemptuous of loving God for selfish reasons since, after all, God has blessed us so much that it is only to be expected that those blessings will elicit love from us.

But, Bernard said, the ideal is for us to move beyond this, into the third stage, in which we love God for God's sake: "No longer do we love God because of our [needs], but because we have tasted and seen how gracious the Lord is." The movement from the second to the third stage is made by means of spiritual disciplines: "When [a Christian] has learned to worship God and to seek Him aright, meditating on God, reading God's Word, praying and obeying His commandments, he comes gradually to know what God is, and finds Him altogether lovely."

Bernard felt that Christians who reach the third stage must remain in it for a long time; in fact, he thought that it was almost impossible for anyone to move to the fourth stage in the present life, though perhaps some special

Christians such as martyrs have done so.

The fourth stage is the love of oneself for God's sake alone. By this Bernard meant the mystical vision of God in which one's love of oneself is no longer distinguishable from one's love of God. Here Bernard appealed to an idea that originated in 2 Peter and that in the early and medieval church was treasured as one of the most popular ways of presenting the fullness of salvation. The idea was that Christians "become participants in the divine nature" (2 Peter 1:4).

Bernard understood the fourth stage to be an experience that happens to Christians after they die, in which their lives are so taken up into God's life that their love for themselves becomes a love for God. In more Protestant terms, this is similar to Charles Wesley's assertion in his hymn "Love Divine, All Loves Excelling" that in heaven all Christians will be "lost in wonder, love, and praise."[7]

If we agree that the fourth stage is reserved for the life to come, we can see that Bernard's first three stages are accurate descriptions of a Christian's journey through life: from selfish love of self, to selfish love of God, to unselfish love of God.

There are many ways of mapping our journey through life, ways that take account of the particularities of all our lives, and Bernard's is just one example. The important thing is not which map of our journey we use; the important thing is to be aware that we are moving forward in our journey as Christians.

WE WILL ARRIVE AT HOME

The third and final thing to be said about the pilgrimage is that there is a destination and that we will eventually reach it. We may think about our destination in terms of God and in terms of ourselves.

In the *New English Bible* Romans 11:36 reads as follows: "Source, Guide, and Goal of all that is—to him be glory for ever!" We Christians have tended to emphasize that God is the source or creator of all things, and that God guides us throughout our lives, but we have tended to place less emphasis on the fact that God also is the destiny toward whom we are moving. Perhaps we have not wanted to risk minimizing the reality that God is present with us now. For whatever reason, the idea that in the life to come we will know God more fully than in this life is sometimes missing from our understanding.

But there can be no doubt that it played an important role in the life of the first century church. For example, Paul wrote, "Now we see in a mirror, dimly, but then we will see face to face. Now I know only in part; then I will know fully, even as I have been fully known" (1 Corinthians 13:12). In describing our destination John wrote, "His servants will worship him; they will see his face, and his name will be on their foreheads" (Revelation 22:3–4). Since we have come from God (by creation) and are moving toward God (by salvation), then our final destiny will in fact be the same as our origin, namely, God.

G.K. Chesterton has written about how an origin

sometimes turns out to be a destiny:

I have often had a fancy for writing a romance about an English yachtsman who slightly miscalculated his course and discovered England under the impression that it was a new island in the South Seas.... I am that man in a yacht.... I am the man who with the utmost daring discovered what had been discovered before.... I discovered that it was orthodoxy.[8]

Chesterton was thinking about beliefs in this life, and our interest right now is with the life to come, but his metaphor helps us see the point. A few years later T.S. Eliot was speaking of the future when he wrote:

We shall not cease from exploration
And the end of all our exploring
Will be to arrive where we started
And know the place for the first time.[9]

Pilgrims return to the God from whom they began their journey.

At present we are in the position of children going on a trip to a place they have never been before. They cannot imagine what it will be like: "We see in a mirror, dimly" (1 Corinthians 13:12). When we finally arrive, we shall experience both wonder and welcome as we find God even more glorious than we are able to imagine now.

We can also say that our destiny is to become good

people; the conventional way to express this is to say that in heaven we shall be glorified. This means that the relationship between our lives now and our lives then will be one of both continuity and discontinuity. We will still be the persons we are, but we will also be changed. The change is mysterious and full of promise. John wrote, "What we do know is this: when he is revealed, we will be like him, for we will see him as he is" (1 John 3:2). We cannot understand how God will bring about such a transformation, and we cannot understand exactly what we shall be like, but we live in hope that we will be delivered forever from our natural selfishness and that we will never again fail to love God and to love those around us.

Whether we describe this in Bernard's terms—love of the self for God's sake—or in some other, clearly it is our very great hope, and this hope can support us during the moments in our lives when we face discouraging experiences.

CONCLUSION

Christians have a love-hate relationship with the world. We love the world God created, which God has entrusted to the care of human beings, the world whose heavens declare the glory of God, the world where "there lives the dearest freshness deep down things."[10] But in this world things are not the way they're supposed to be, and we live here as expatriates and travelers. Our homeland is scarcely imaginable to us now, but every day that we live we travel

137

one day closer to it. We are journeying toward a city "whose architect and builder is God." We don't know where it is, but we'll know it when we get there.

CHAPTER 7

"You are...
a royal priesthood."

—1 Peter 2:9

Priest

All Christians are priests, but very few Christians think of themselves as priests. Christians in the Episcopal Church and the Roman Catholic Church may find it difficult to think of themselves as priests because there is within their churches a group of persons who have been set aside to serve as priests. Christians in churches that do not have a set-aside group of priests tend to think of their churches as not having priests at all. So far as I'm aware, there is no church in which members naturally think of themselves as priests.

Yet, as we shall see, the New Testament

clearly teaches that all Christians are priests. Before we look at that, however, we will give some attention to the background for that teaching; this will make the teaching more meaningful to us.

PRIESTS IN THE OLD TESTAMENT

At the beginning of the story of the covenant people of God, there was no group of persons who were set apart to function as priests. The principal act of worship was the offering of sacrifices, mostly animal sacrifices. Sacrifices were offered by the heads of families or of clans in Israel, men such as Abraham, Isaac, and Jacob.

Jacob had twelve sons; one of them was named Levi. During the period of the Exodus, the Lord gave instructions saying that the male descendants of Levi were to serve as priests on behalf of the entire nation. When the people entered Canaan, the land was to be divided up among the descendants of eleven of the sons of Jacob, but the descendants of Levi were given no land to farm (see Joshua 18:7). The Levites were to receive their income from the people for their service of leading the people in the worship of God, just as many Christian ministers today receive their income from leading churches.

The priesthood in Israel was therefore hereditary; people were not called to be priests, they were born to be priests.

Apparently during the period of the judges the tribe of Levi did not lead the nation in sacrificial worship.

Presumably the reason for this was that, prior to King David and King Solomon, Israel did not have a central place of worship, and the people offered sacrifices to the Lord at various locations such as Shechem and Shiloh.

About 1000 B.C., King David made Jerusalem his capital, and soon after that his son Solomon built the first Temple in Jerusalem. Solomon began the process of centralizing Israel's sacrificial worship there; this process was carried much further by King Josiah in the seventh century before Christ.

The priestly caste served as a stable force in Israel's religious life. They taught the Torah to the people, and, most important of all, they led the people in the worship of God by means of animal sacrifices. As Moses had said of them in a prayer, "They teach Jacob your ordinances, and Israel your law; they place incense before you, and whole burnt offerings on your altar" (Deuteronomy 33:10).

At some time in Israel's history, a distinction began to be made between the work of priests who had descended from Aaron (Aaron and Moses were brothers and were of the tribe of Levi) and other descendants of Levi who were not descended from Aaron (see Exodus 28:1). By the New Testament era, the people called priests were all descendants of Aaron and were the dominant group, and the Levites were a lesser group, perhaps providing support for the work of the priests.

Two Promises
in the Old Testament

That is the story of priests in the Old Testament: a small group of males who were descended from Levi (and later Aaron) was set aside to serve as priests, and they led Israel's sacrificial worship and taught the people of Israel the Torah.

However, the Old Testament also contains two passages in which the Lord promised Israel that in the future there would be a change in the priesthood. The passages are found in Exodus 19 and Isaiah 61.

In Exodus 19 the Lord tells Moses that at some time in the future, the covenant people themselves will be priests; here is the passage:

Now therefore, if you obey my voice and keep my covenant, you shall be my treasured possession out of all the peoples. Indeed, the whole earth is mine, but you shall be for me a priestly kingdom and a holy nation.

—Exodus 19:5–6

This was an extraordinary promise. When it was fulfilled, it would bring about a transformation in the religious life of God's people. No longer would there be a hereditary caste of priests to lead God's people in sacrificial worship and to teach the Torah; instead, all God's people would do these things.

And apparently, they would do them for the entire

world. Just as the priests were a group within the covenant people who served all the covenant people, so the covenant people would be a group within the human race who would serve the entire human race. This becomes more evident in the passage in Isaiah in which the promise to the covenant people is reaffirmed:

Strangers shall stand and feed your flocks, foreigners shall till your land and dress your vines; but you shall be called priests of the LORD, you shall be named ministers of our God; you shall enjoy the wealth of the nations, and in their riches you shall glory.

—Isaiah 61:5–6

This promise meant that what the priests have been doing on behalf of Israel, all of Israel would someday do on behalf of the entire world. Just as the priests had taught the Torah to the covenant people, so the covenant people would teach the Torah to the world. And as the priests had offered sacrifices to God on behalf of the covenant people, so the covenant people would offer sacrifices to God on behalf of the world.

These two passages are about the responsibilities and privileges of priests. In Exodus 19, the promise was presented to Moses as a great responsibility. When God makes all the covenant people priests, they will all bear the weighty responsibilities that up until then were borne only by the elite group of priests.

In Isaiah 61, the promise was presented to the prophet

as both a responsibility and a privilege. Where Exodus had emphasized the responsibility that the covenant people would bear as priests of God, Isaiah emphasized the privilege and benefits they would experience as priests of God.

Responsibility and privilege: that is the content of the Old Testament promises about the priesthood of all God's people.

FULFILLMENT IN THE NEW TESTAMENT

The promises found in Exodus 19 and Isaiah 61 were not fulfilled in the Old Testament era. When the New Testament era opened, Israel's worship was still led by the elite caste of male priests and Levites. The Gospels contain several stories about Jesus dealing with priests and Levites, and in some of them the priests were unfriendly to Jesus.

This is the background for the most important of all biblical passages about the priesthood of all God's people. It is found in 1 Peter:

Come to him, a living stone, though rejected by mortals yet chosen and precious in God's sight, and like living stones, let yourselves be built into a spiritual house, to be a holy priesthood, to offer spiritual sacrifices acceptable to God through Jesus Christ.... you are a chosen race, a royal priesthood, a holy nation, God's own people, in order that you may proclaim the mighty acts of him who called you out of darkness into his marvelous light.

—1 Peter 2:4–9

In this classic passage Peter twice asserted that the promises that God had given to Israel through Moses and Isaiah had been fulfilled in the Christian community; in this new people of God, all members are priests of the Lord.

It is principally on the authority of 1 Peter 2 that we Christians today believe that all of us who are believers in Jesus are priests of God. Our priesthood is confirmed in three passages in Revelation in which John casually refers to Christians as priests. John said that Jesus "loves us and freed us from our sins by his blood, and made us to be a kingdom, priests serving his God and Father" (Revelation 1:5–6). He recorded a prayer in which the elders sing to God about the saints, "You have made them to be a kingdom and priests serving our God" (Revelation 5:10). He said of those whom God raises from the dead, "They will be priests of God and of Christ, and they will reign with him a thousand years" (Revelation 20:6).

CHRISTIAN SACRIFICE

These are the only passages in which the word *priests* is used of all Christians, but the New Testament teaching about priesthood is not restricted to these passages. We have seen that throughout Israel's history there was one activity that was reserved for priests. That was the activity of offering sacrifices to God. Therefore, all of the New Testament passages that speak about Christians offering sacrifices are in fact speaking about the priesthood of Christians.

What we see in this story about priests is a spiritualizing of priesthood. In the Old Testament era there was a caste of literal priests who offered literal animal sacrifices to God, but in the New Testament all of God's people are spiritually rather than literally priests who offer spiritual rather than literal sacrifices to God.

The New Testament Christians did not offer animal sacrifices to God. They were, in fact, the only people in the Roman world we know of who did not offer animal sacrifices, at least until 70 A.D. At that time the Temple in Jerusalem was destroyed once again and the Jews stopped offering animal sacrifices to God.

But the Christians had stopped offering animal sacrifices before 70 A.D. Their rationale for not offering animal sacrifices was extraordinary. They believed that when Jesus died on the cross, He offered a final, perfect sacrifice to God, so that there was no longer any need for animal sacrifices.

The first Christians were of course Jews, and, though as Christians they did not offer animal sacrifices, they struggled with whether or not to continue offering the traditional Jewish sacrifices. After all, the sacrifices were commanded in the Torah, and the Torah was the Word of God. At least some of the early Christians continued to attend Jewish worship services and presumably to offer sacrifices, Paul among them. On the other hand, we also have a hint in Hebrews 6 of an unnamed Christian leader urging his readers not continue to offer animal sacrifices in the

Temple. In the second generation the issue was settled when Christians were no longer welcome at Jewish worship either in the Temple or in the synagogues.

Though the Christians themselves never offered animal sacrifices in their worship services, from the beginning they did offer spiritual sacrifices to God. In doing this they were following an ancient tradition of Israel that called God's people to offer spiritual sacrifices. A classic example of this appears in Psalm 51, which is by David. David had sinned terribly against the Lord, committing adultery and murder. The prophet Nathan had confronted David about his sin, and David had immediately repented. It would have been conventional for David to arrange for an animal sacrifice to be offered to atone for his sins, but he didn't do that. Instead, according to tradition, he wrote these words: "You have no delight in sacrifice; if I were to give a burnt offering, you would not be pleased. The sacrifice acceptable to God is a broken spirit; a broken and a contrite heart, O God, you will not despise" (Psalm 51:16–17). David offered that spiritual sacrifice to God.

Insights such as this helped God's people to begin to think about sacrifices in spiritual terms rather than in terms of literal animal offerings. The early Christians who affirmed the priesthood of all believers taught that all believers are to offer spiritual sacrifices to God. Peter said exactly that: we are "to be a holy priesthood, to offer spiritual sacrifices acceptable to God through Jesus Christ" (1 Peter 2:5).

THREE SPIRITUAL SACRIFICES

What are spiritual sacrifices? We will consider three that are mentioned in the New Testament.

Paul wrote to the Romans: "I appeal to you therefore, brothers and sisters, by the mercies of God, to present your bodies as a living sacrifice, holy and acceptable to God, which is your spiritual worship" (Romans 12:1). Paul taught that when Christians devote their lives to God, that is effectively the offering of a sacrifice of spiritual worship to God. Our lives are God's gift to us; the way we live our lives are our offering back to God. This is a priestly task, and it is one that all Christians are called to carry out.

The force of Paul's appeal is that Christians should make this sacrificial offering because of God's mercies, that is, because God has been so gracious to them. His argument is that the only reasonable thing for people who have experienced God's love given in Jesus to do is to worship God, and the spiritual worship that God wants from those people is the sacrifice of their own lives.

This is a sacrifice that every Christ follower can offer to God. It is a good idea for us to offer it repeatedly, just as the priests of the Old Testament era repeatedly offered sacrifices to the Lord.

For various reasons we tend to imagine that it is difficult to offer ourselves to God, but there is a sense in which it is not difficult. That is, it is possible in just a minute or two for us to pause and to reflect on what Christ has done for us, and then to say from our hearts, *Lord, I give You my life as a living sacrifice.*

How often should we do this? Perhaps the ideal would be daily, but certainly waiting more than a week to do it can't be good for us spiritually. A good time to do it is when we are engaged in worshiping the Lord along with our fellow Christians on Sunday.

So, the first spiritual sacrifice we offer to God is our lives. The author of Hebrews mentions two other sacrifices: "Through [Jesus], then, let us continually offer a sacrifice of praise to God, that is, the fruit of lips that confess his name. Do not neglect to do good and to share what you have, for such sacrifices are pleasing to God" (Hebrews 13:15–16).

The two sacrifices mentioned in this passage are praise to God and sharing with others. It is our priestly responsibility to offer regularly the sacrifice of worship to God. That is one of the principal reasons Christians meet each Sunday. In church, led by musicians and others, Christians unite their hearts in offering to God the sacrifice of worship and praise. They do not kill any animals, but as a community of priests they all offer to the Lord the important sacrifice of worship.

When we think about going to church, it is natural for us to think about what we get from it. I don't think there is anything wrong with this. We all need help in our lives, and we should pay attention to whether or not we are getting the help we need from church.

But in church we are not only getting; we are also

giving. Christians go to worship services in order to give something to God, namely, the worship and praise that are due unto God. It is right for them to do this, and it is important that they do it.

Sometimes Christians tend to think about going to church in the way they think about going to a theater. The ministers and the choir are the actors, the congregation is the audience, and the congregation comes to church to see how well the actors will do. But there is another way to think about going to church, a way that takes seriously the priesthood of all believers. It is to realize that the Lord is the audience and that all of us, congregation and ministers and choir, are the actors. Together we all, as priests, offer our worship to the Lord, and the Lord receives that offering from us.

The other kind of sacrifice is a surprise. The author of Hebrews says that when Christians help other people, and when they share what they have with other people, those are sacrifices to God (Hebrews 13:16).

Christians don't usually think this way, but it would be good for us if we began to train ourselves to do so. It can help us to do good things for other people if we understand that good works are a form of worship that God expects from us. We help people because we care for them; we help them also because God values what we do for them.

One of the ways Christians share with others is by giving financial support to their churches. The church then uses the money to help people in various ways. This means that one important way we do our priestly work of helping others is by supporting the church financially.

And this explains the curious fact, not often commented on, that it is customary to refer to the collecting of the money during a church service as *taking an offering.* The word *offering* is a reference to offering a sacrifice to God. Christians offer their money to be used to carry out the spiritual sacrifice of helping people. This means that when we put money in the offering plate, we are doing two things simultaneously: we are taking a practical step to help the church pay its bills and carry out its ministries, and we are offering a sacrifice of worship to God.

The idea that giving to those in need is effectively giving to God is found in various places in the Bible. For example, we considered earlier the verse from Proverbs that says: "When you give to the poor, it is like lending to the LORD, and the LORD will pay you back" (Proverbs 19:17 TEV). And in Jesus' great message about the final judgment (Matthew 25:31–46) He said, "Just as you did it to one of the least of these who are members of my family, you did it to me" (25:40). The writer of Hebrews was thinking along the same lines when he wrote that sharing with others is a sacrifice that pleases God.

Here, then, are three spiritual sacrifices that all Christians may offer to God: our lives, our worship, and our care for the poor and needy.

Are there others? Doubtless there are, and it would be a good spiritual exercise for each of us to reflect on the question, "What spiritual sacrifices might I offer to God at this time in my life?"

TWO OTHER PRIESTLY RESPONSIBILITIES

The offering of sacrifices is the most distinctive work of priests, but it is not the only work, and we will give attention now to two other priestly tasks. Peter mentioned one when he wrote that Christians are "a royal priesthood... in order that you may proclaim the mighty acts of him who called you out of darkness into his marvelous light" (1 Peter 2:9).

Israel's priests taught the Torah to the people, and Christians who teach the message of the Bible to others are carrying out a priestly function, too. Christians do this at many levels, from informal witness, to instructing children in Sunday school classes, to teaching adult Bible studies, to providing graduate studies in Bible in universities and seminaries. In all of this the priesthood of all Christians is important; the church would be impoverished if it allowed a scholarly caste to co-opt all Bible teaching and Christian witness. While we are grateful for the help that scholars of the Bible can give to the rest of us, the responsibility for teaching the Bible rests with all Christians, not just with the scholars.

Israel's worship of God also included prayer, as Christian worship does, and Christians who offer prayers to God, especially prayers on behalf of the world, are performing a priestly task.

Paul was speaking of this kind of priestly work when he urged "that supplications, prayers, intercessions, and thanksgivings be made for everyone, for kings and all who are in high positions, so that we may lead a quiet and peaceable life in all godliness and dignity" (1 Timothy 2:1–2). Of course, in the first century the kings would have been pagans, not Christians, so Paul was telling Timothy to pray for pagan leaders who, because they were pagans, were unable to pray to the true and living God for themselves, yet who, because they were political leaders, needed God's help. When Christians today pray for the world, including those in the world who do not have a personal knowledge of the true and living God, they are functioning as priests.

In 1989 I had an experience that gave me a clearer understanding of how we Christians may serve as priests by praying for the world. It was in October, and I had flown to California to give some lectures at Golden Gate Baptist Theological Seminary in Mill Valley, across the bay from San Francisco. Just before suppertime a magnitude 7.1 earthquake struck the Bay Area; it was the worst earthquake since 1906. Sixty-two people were killed, more than 3700 were hurt, the Oakland Bay Bridge collapsed, and the damage to property totaled almost $3 billion. Over in Mill Valley we were safe; we felt the quake, and there was slight damage, but not much. When it was dark, we could see the fires across the bay in San Francisco.

When we gathered the next morning in a chapel service, we all wanted to know what we could do to help the hurting people in San Francisco. Was there anything we could do about the fires, or about people who were homeless, or about the looting that had begun?

The answer was yes and no. No, we could not enter the city of San Francisco; officials there had told outsiders to stay away in order to allow the fire and police and health departments to do their work efficiently.

But, yes, there was something we could do. We on the seminary campus could take up our role as priests on behalf of the world. We could pray for people who were hurting from the effects of the earthquake, some of whom might not know how to pray for themselves. So we did, as a community of priests; we prayed for all of the people of San Francisco, some of whom were our sisters and brothers in the Christian faith, and others who were not. We tried to discharge our priestly responsibility to pray for the world.

In the Book of Common Prayer of the Anglican Church there is a beautiful prayer that seems to me to be ideal when Christians pray for the world: "Open, O Lord, the eyes of all people to behold thy gracious hand in all thy works."[1] When we Christians include all human beings in our prayers, we are fulfilling part of our priestly responsibilities.

PRIESTLY RESPONSIBILITIES AND PRIVILEGES

Most Christians find it difficult to think of themselves as priests of God, but, since the writers of the New Testament clearly intended us to do just that, Christians should intentionally act to raise their consciousness of this understanding of their lives. All Christians bear the priestly responsibility of offering spiritual sacrifices to God, sacrifices such as their own lives, worship, and giving aid to the poor. They also bear the responsibility of telling the story of God's work in Christ, and the responsibility of praying for people who, because they do not know the Lord, are unable to pray to God for themselves.

Along with these serious responsibilities go great privileges. Since all Christians are priests, all Christians have the privilege of coming to God for themselves. All Christians have the privileges of prayer, and of learning and teaching about the Bible, privileges that some claim belong only to this or that special group.

This is a book about individual Christians, but throughout the book we have seen that it is only as we think of Christians as members of the church that we can understand their lives properly. That is particularly true of the image of priest; there is not a single passage in the Bible that speaks of an individual Christian in the singular as a priest; the Bible always refers to the priesthood of all Christians, in the plural. The priestly responsibilities of offering spiritual sacrifices and teaching the Bible and

155

praying for the world are too heavy to be borne alone; they must be borne in the company of other Christians.

CHRISTIAN FREEDOM

You may have noticed that in this chapter I have not said anything about Christian freedom. That may seem strange to you, since nowadays it is conventional to associate the priesthood of all believers with freedom. Because we are all priests, we are free from the tyranny of a priestly caste that claimed they had control of our access to God, and because we are all priests, we are free to read and interpret the Bible for ourselves.

The association of priesthood with freedom is understandable, but so far as I can tell it is not found in the Bible. None of the passages about priesthood or about sacrifices says anything about freedom. There, the emphasis is on responsibility and privilege.

When, then, did we begin to associate the priesthood of all believers with Christian freedom? It happened, I think, in the sixteenth century, and the person who made it happen was Martin Luther. Luther was a devout Roman Catholic monk and professor of the Bible, but he came to believe that the Roman Catholic Church was losing sight of the gospel. He thought it was wrong for the church to tell people that they could not know God without submitting to the authority of Rome and its clergy. He retrieved the biblical image of the priesthood of all believers and employed it as a device for freeing people from what he perceived to be the tyranny of Roman Catholic priests.

While this is understandable, it is not, I think, biblical, and therefore I have not written about freedom in this chapter.

On the other hand, I do want to mention now that in the New Testament we are told repeatedly that God is profoundly concerned about human freedom. Jesus said that "If the Son makes you free, you will be free indeed" (John 8:36), and Paul urged the Galatian churches, "For freedom Christ has set us free. Stand firm, therefore, and do not submit again to a yoke of bondage" (Galatians 5:1). Christ does indeed give us freedom; He frees us from the need to justify ourselves before God, and He works to free us from our destructive addictions and compulsions; He frees us to trust in God and to love God and to live without the sort of fear of death and fear of God that most human beings have experienced across the millennia. He set "free those who all their lives were held in slavery by the fear of death" (Hebrews 2:15).

Freedom is important to us as Christians, and we are deeply grateful for the freedom of Christ. We also are grateful for the responsibilities and privileges that are ours as priests of God.

CHAPTER 8

"We are children of God."

—Romans 8:16

Child

eaders are apt to have the opposite reaction to the image in this chapter than they did to the previous one. It is difficult and rare for Christians to think of ourselves as priests; it is easy and customary for us to think of ourselves as God's children. In fact, we are so accustomed to thinking of ourselves as God's children that we may resist the suggestion that child is an image for a Christian at all; instead we might think, "These others may be images, but we *are really* God's children."

While that's understandable, it's misleading.

After all, we *are really* disciples, servants, stewards, soldiers, athletes, travelers, and priests of God as well as children of God. Of course, we are not literally soldiers and so on, but we are not literally children of God, either; we are literally children of two human beings, our biological parents, and some of us are literally children of our adoptive parents. We are really and truly, but spiritually rather than literally, children of God.

CHILDREN OF GOD IN THE OLD TESTAMENT

Though it is conventional nowadays for the people of God to think of themselves as God's children, this has not always been the case. In the Old Testament era it was more conventional for the covenant people to think of their nation as a single child of God. "Thus says the LORD: Israel is my firstborn son" (Exodus 4:22). Through Hosea the Lord said, "When Israel was a child, I loved him, and out of Egypt I called my son" (Hosea 11:1).

The Old Testament contains a few passages that speak of all the covenant people as God's children rather than as God's child. For example, Moses said, "You are children of the LORD your God" (Deuteronomy 14:1), and Jeremiah wrote, "Return, O faithless children, says the LORD" (Jeremiah 3:14).

Occasionally it is said that it is those members of the covenant people who faithfully keep the covenant who are God's children: "As a father has compassion for his children, so the LORD has compassion for those who fear him" (Psalm 103:13).

There are a few other passages in the Old Testament that speak of God's having a child, and they are about kings of Israel. For example, the Lord said about Solomon: "I will be a father to him, and he shall be a son to me" (2 Samuel 7:14). Many scholars believe that Psalm 2 was a coronation psalm used in ceremonies launching the reigns of the kings of Israel. In that psalm the Lord says: "I have set my king on Zion, my holy hill." Then the king says: "I will tell of the decree of the LORD: He said to me, 'You are my son; today I have begotten you'" (Psalm 2:6–7).

The Old Testament teaching about children of God is wonderful, but in it the idea that God is Father and that each of God's people is a child of God is very limited compared with the New Testament teaching.

JESUS AND THE FATHER

It is Jesus who first emphasized the fact that God is Father. There is a parallel in Jesus' teachings to the two groups of sayings in the Old Testament, God as Father of the king and God as Father of the nation: Jesus spoke of God as His own Father and of God as Father of His followers. He was careful to distinguish these two ideas, sometimes speaking of "your Father" (for examples, Matthew 5:16, 5:45, 6:1) and sometimes speaking of "my Father" (Matthew 7:21, 10:32–33, 11:27). Jesus spoke often of God as His Father; in fact, every recorded prayer of Jesus, with one exception, begins with the word "Father" (the exception is found in Matthew 27:46).

The writers of the New Testament followed Jesus' example and carefully distinguished between the way in which Jesus is the Son of God and the way in which Jesus' followers are children of God. Here are five of the ways in which the authors of the New Testament expressed the uniqueness of the relationship between Jesus the Son and God the Father.

First, Jesus was God's Son in that He had no biological father. When Jesus was born to Mary, who was a virgin, an angel told Joseph, "He will be called the Son of God" (Luke 1:35).

Second, in the Gospel of John, Jesus is called Son (Greek, *huios*) of God; John reserves the word *huios* for Jesus and uses another word altogether for Christians; they are *teknoi*, children of God.

Third, John said that Jesus was God's *monogenes huios*, God's one-and-only, or only begotten, Son: "God so loved the world, that he gave his only begotten Son" (John 3:16 KJV).

Fourth, in the Gospels God says of Jesus: "This is my Son, the Beloved, with whom I am well pleased" (Matthew 3:17; see also Luke 9:35).

Fifth and finally, both John and Paul spoke of the fact that God the Father sent Jesus into the world. "God did not send the Son into the world to condemn the world, but in order that the world might be saved through him" (John 3:17). "When the fullness of time had come, God sent his

Son, born of a woman, born under the law, in order to redeem those who were under the law" (Galatians 4:4–5). "God sent his only Son into the world so that we might live through him" (1 John 4:9). Perhaps these writers had in mind Jesus' parable about a king who sent his son back home to collect produce from his vineyard (see Mark 12:1–11).

None of this language about Jesus would be used about human beings as God's children. Clearly, therefore, Jesus and the writers of the New Testament believed that Jesus was a unique Son of God.

CHRISTIANS ARE CHILDREN OF GOD

This makes it all the more remarkable that they also believed so firmly that Christians are children of God. But they certainly believed that also, and once again it was Jesus who emphasized the fact.

Perhaps the single most important thing Jesus did to ensure that His followers would think of themselves a children of God was to tell them: "Pray then in this way: Our Father" (Matthew 6:9). As a result of this instruction, hundreds of millions of Christians across almost 2000 years have found it natural to begin their prayers with the words, "Our Father." That fact alone would insure that Christians would think of themselves as children of God.

The Lord's Prayer is the most influential teaching about God's fatherhood, but it is not the only one. The New Testament contains dozens of references to the fact that

God is the Father of Christ followers. For example, "See what love the Father has given us, that we should be called children of God; and that is what we are....Beloved, we are God's children now" (1 John 3:1–2).

The writers of the New Testament affirmed that Christ followers are children of God both by birth and by adoption. Several New Testament writers spoke of Christians as having been born of God. Jesus told Nicodemus, "You must be born from above" (John 3:7), and John said that all who believed in Jesus "were born...of God" (John 1:13). James said that God "gave us birth by the word of truth" (James 1:18), and Peter wrote that "You have been born anew...through the living and enduring word of God" (1 Peter 1:23).

On the other hand, Paul was the only writer in the New Testament who spoke of Christians as having been adopted by God. He did so on three occasions. To the Romans he wrote: "You did not receive a spirit of slavery to fall back into fear, but you have received a spirit of adoption. When we cry, 'Abba! Father!' it is that very Spirit bearing witness with our spirit that we are children of God" (Romans 8:15–16). In his letter to the churches of Galatia, Paul combined a statement about Jesus as God's unique Son with a statement about the adoption of Jesus' followers to be children of God: "When the fullness of time had come, God sent his Son, born of a woman, born under the law, in order to redeem those who were under the law, so that we might receive adoption as children. And because you are children, God has sent the Spirit of his Son into our hearts, crying 'Abba! Father!'" (Galatians 4:4–6). And to the Ephesians Paul wrote, "He destined us for adoption as his children through Jesus Christ" (Ephesians 1:5).

The themes of birth and adoption both suggest important things about ourselves. The new birth suggests that we are new creations of God with a fresh start in life, and it suggests that we have ties with God that are unbreakable in the way blood ties between parents and their biological children are unbreakable. Adoption suggests that God has intentionally chosen to make us His children, just as adoptive parents intentionally choose to bring children into their family and home.

A RARE USE OF THE IMAGE OF CHILD

So far we have observed four uses of the image of child. First, Israel is God's son. Second, King Solomon and his successors were God's sons. Third, Jesus is God's unique, only-begotten Son. Fourth, each one of Jesus' followers is a child of God.

There is a fifth use of the image of child. It is rare in the Bible, but we will note it briefly. It appears clearly in Hebrews 2. The author has just presented the idea that Jesus is superior to angels, and that has created a difficulty for Him; if Jesus is greater than angels, then can He really be fully identified with human beings in such a way as to act as a priest on their behalf? The writer was fully convinced that priests must be closely identified with those on behalf of whom they offer sacrifices:

For the one who sanctifies and those who are sanctified all have one Father. For this reason Jesus is not ashamed to call them brothers and sisters.... Since, therefore, the children share flesh and blood, he himself likewise shared the same things.... it is clear that he did not come to help angels, but the descendants of Abraham. Therefore he had to become like his brothers and sisters in every respect.

—Hebrews 2:11–17

In this striking passage, all human beings are said to be children of God, and brothers and sisters of Jesus. The distinction between this rare use of the child image and its use to refer to Christians is expressed nicely in the following statement: "God is Father in truth to those who become children of God through faith in Jesus Christ. He is fatherly in His attitude toward all men."[1]

Our concern in this book is, of course, for the fact that every follower of Jesus is a child of God, and we will turn our attention now to that fact.

THE FAITH OF CHILDREN

What do Christians do because they are God's children?

In the New Testament we find several answers to this question. Matthew tells us two stories that display Jesus' attitudes toward and feelings about children. In one of them (Matthew 19:13–15) Jesus was asked to bless some children. Giving a blessing to children involved laying hands on them, and it was a practice that was taken very seriously in the world of the Bible; see, for example, Genesis 48. The disciples tried to keep the children away from Jesus, but Jesus didn't like that; He said to them, "Let the little children come to me, and do not stop them; for it is to such as these that the kingdom of heaven belongs" (Matthew 19:14).

In the other story (Matthew 18:1–14) Jesus' disciples asked Jesus who would be the greatest person in the Kingdom of heaven. Jesus replied by calling a little child and saying to the disciples, "Whoever becomes humble like this child is the greatest in the kingdom of heaven" (Matthew 18:4).

What did Jesus see in children that He so valued? Here is how Malcolm O. Tolbert, one of our great scholars of the New Testament, answers that question:

What does it mean to "humble" one's self like a child? The child is a good figure for a kingdom person because he is totally dependent. If he is to survive at all, he must depend on his parents for food, clothing, and care. He cannot provide for himself. This is the basic idea in humility. The humble person recognizes his absolute dependence upon God. His security and his future depend on the love and care of his Father. The greatest disciple, therefore, is not the proud man who is always comparing his talents and accomplishments with those of his brothers to their disadvantage. The greatest disciple is the one who is most aware of his limitations and contingencies, who is most aware that everything he has is given, and who is acutely conscious that he has a future only because God guarantees it.[2]

I quoted this passage at length because I believe Dr. Tolbert pointed to the precise thing that Jesus so valued in the lives of children, their humble dependence on their parents.

The moral for Christians is clear: we are to have a humble dependence upon our Father. We can move toward humble dependence by reflecting upon our origins (we did not create ourselves) and on our salvation (we did not save ourselves); our very being, and our new being in Christ, are gifts of God. Our past and present and future are all gifts of God; we exist and live today because our Father wants us to exist and to live. Humble, dependent people recognize that.

THE INNOCENCE OF CHILDREN

In his letter to the church at Philippi, Paul named one of the things that he valued in the lives of children: "Do all things without murmuring and arguing, so that you may be blameless and innocent, children of God without blemish" (Philippians 2:14–15). Paul was urging Christians to imitate the innocence of children.

Our initial response to this may be to ask whether it is even possible for adults who have seen the raw side of life ever to achieve the innocence of children. It is difficult, but presumably it is not impossible since, if it were impossible,

Paul would not have urged Christians to do it.

If you are like me, you may be able to identify some persons of your acquaintance who have been faithful children of God for so long that they have become very, very good people. While they still make mistakes in their lives, they no longer act rebelliously or maliciously.

The great church leader of the eighteenth century, John Wesley, spoke of this state of affairs as perfection. The word *perfection* has troubled many Christians, but Wesley's conviction that Christians could arrive at this state matches what Paul wrote to the Philippians. Wesley taught that there are stages in Christian life ranging from newborn to maturity.[3] He thought that mature Christians love God so deeply that they no longer deliberately rebel against God. They still make mistakes in relationships, in understanding, and even in moral judgment, but they no longer actively resist God in their lives; they have become, in Paul's words, "blameless and innocent, children of God without blemish." These people still need God's grace and help in their lives, they still need to struggle against temptations, and they still need to grow as Christians. But their lives display a childlike quality of innocence that should be the goal of all Christians.

While many of us are uncomfortable with the word *perfection* and with the assertion that it is possible for a Christian to arrive at perfection, I think that all of us should have as a goal that we become "blameless and innocent, children of God."

THE TALK OF CHILDREN

So far we have considered two qualities of children that we are to imitate: humble dependence upon our Father and a childlike innocence that comes from loving the Father so much that we no longer rebel against Him. What else in the lives of children should be present in the lives of Christians?

It is characteristic of children that, once they have learned to talk, they talk to their parents. It would be tragic if a child did not communicate with her parents, and barring some special circumstance, that does not happen with young children (it is not unusual for adolescent children to go through a stage in which they are not communicative with their parents).

It is natural for children to expect their parents to love them and to listen to them because they love them, and they expect that their parents ordinarily will be responsive to what they say.

When God's children talk to their Father, that is called prayer. As we have seen, Jesus told His followers, when they pray, to say "Our Father" (Matthew 6:9). This is, in my judgment, the most important guidance ever given to us concerning prayer. In order to follow the spirit of Jesus' instructions, Christians must think of God as their Father and of themselves as God's children, and then they must talk to God in something like the way in which children talk to their parents. This means that they are to trust God to listen and to be responsive to their prayers.

Prayer is talking to God, who listens and responds because He loves us. This is the children's view of prayer, and they understand prayer in this way because this is what they do with their parents.

I believe that the children's view of prayer is true. There are other understandings of prayer which, some argue, are more mature; for example, prayer may take the form of meditating on a Bible text, or it may take the contemplative form of sitting silently in God's presence. Both meditation and contemplation are appropriate Christian practices, and millions of Christians have practiced them and been helped by them. All that I am asking here is that, in our enthusiasm for these forms of prayer, we should not be dismissive of childlike prayer. To do so would be to overlook Jesus' teaching and to miss out on a natural and important component of our lives as Christians.

The great theoretical question about prayer is, does it make a difference to God? Christians know that prayer helps them; there is no doubt about that. But does prayer matter to God? The answer becomes evident if we ask, does what children say to their loving parents matter to the parents?

The answer is that it surely does. It is not that children manipulate or control their parents; mature parents will never allow that to happen. But parents are, in fact, responsive to what their children say to them. And God is, in fact, responsive to what Christians say in their prayers.

My wife Caroline and I have two children, Stephanie

and Kenneth. They are both adults now, but when they were small, I learned something important about prayer from observing them. I noticed that our relationships with our children fell into three categories. First, there were some things we gave our children that they had not asked for; for example, when they were very young we began to give them allowances. Second, there were some things they asked for that we did not give them; for example, when Kenneth was very young he wanted a motorcycle; of course, we didn't give him a motorcycle because it was too dangerous for a small child. Third, there were some things that, if our children asked us for them, we gave them what they requested, but if they didn't ask, we didn't give them those things. For example, Stephanie went to camp for a week one summer when she was about twelve years old, and she enjoyed it. When Kenneth got to be about the same age, we didn't suggest that he go to camp, but we waited to see if he would ask; eventually he did ask, and we arranged for him to go to camp, too. The reason we didn't suggest camp was that we didn't want him to get the feeling that we were unhappy having him at home in the summers.

I think that these three relationships exist between the children of God and their Father. First, God gives us some things we never ask for; for these we simply need to be grateful. Second, we ask God for some things and God does not grant our requests; this is sometimes difficult to understand, even painful, but we realize that good parents sometimes say *no* to their children, and the best thing we can do is to accept God's *no* with trust that God knows what is best in the long run. Third, there are things that, if we ask God for them, God gives them to us, but if we do not ask, God does not give them. Prayer really makes a difference to God.

Where does that leave us? If we knew the differences between the three categories of requests, we would pray only about the third, but we don't know the difference. What we do, therefore, is simply to talk to God about what is on our hearts. We ask God for what seems best to us, and we trust God to do what is best. In short, we talk to God as children talk to their parents, confident that God loves us and hears us and responds to us, trusting God to know what is best.

A question that concerns many people is what to say in prayer. Once again, the answer becomes clear if we remember that Christians are God's children and that God is their Father. What do children talk about to their loving parents? Two things. First, they talk about whatever is on their minds: baseball, bicycles, video games, Sunday school, clothes, television, school, and so on. Second, children eventually grow up to share in and to talk about the adult concerns of their parents: their education, their careers, caring for the poor, the nature of leadership, books, ideas, theater, and so on.

So it is when God's children talk to God. First, we talk about whatever is on our minds: protection when we travel, leadership for decisions, comfort when we are grieving, and so on. Second, we talk to God about God's concerns.

Both of these kinds of prayers appear in the Lord's Prayer. The Lord's Prayer contains six requests. The last three requests are about things that are on our minds: daily bread, forgiveness for sins, and deliverance from evil. The first three requests are about God's concerns: that God's name be honored, that God's Kingdom will come, and that God's will be done on earth.

The Lord's Prayer is in fact a series of requests, and children do naturally make requests of their parents. Of course, when children talk to their parents, they do more than make requests, and when God's children talk to God, they do more than make requests, too.

Second, Christians offer worship to God. That is, they express gratitude to God for what God is: loving, good, wise, powerful, and beautiful. Many people believe that worship is the highest form of prayer, and that probably is true, though one should not conclude from that that it would be best to worship without making requests, since to do that would be to suggest that the Lord's Prayer, with its six requests, is an inferior prayer.

One of the ways some Christians deal with the difficulty of finding words for worship is to use written prayers, either from the Bible or from hymns or other devotional literature. Consider, for example, the beautiful and meaningful worship of the following hymn:

Joyful, joyful, we adore Thee, God of glory, Lord of love;
Hearts unfold like flowers before Thee,
Opening to the sun above.
Melt the clouds of sin and sadness,
Drive the dark of doubt away;
Giver of immortal gladness, Fill us with the light of day!

All thy works with joy surround Thee,
Earth and heaven reflect Thy rays,
Stars and angels sing around Thee, Center of unbroken praise.
Field and forest, vale and mountain,
Flowery meadow, flashing sea,
Singing bird and flowing fountain Call us to rejoice in Thee.

Thou art giving and forgiving, ever blessing, ever blest,
Wellspring of the joy of living, ocean depth of happy rest!
Thou our Father, Christ our Brother—
All who live in love are Thine,
Teach us how to love each other, Lift us to the joy divine.[4]

The hymn is filled with the worship of the "God of glory, Lord of love" who is "giving and forgiving, ever blessing, ever blessed." In the last two lines the hymn writer identifies God as our Father and Christ as our brother, and he requests that God will teach us to love and fill our hearts with God's own joy.

Third, Christians offer thanks to God for things God has done. Thanksgiving is similar to worship, but not identical; in worship Christians praise God for what God is, and in thanksgiving they praise God for what God has done. Interestingly, though these two forms of prayer are similar, it is difficult to find words for worship but easy to find words for thanksgiving. All you have to do to offer thanksgiving is to recite the things God has done for you: *Thank You, Lord, for creating me. Thank You for preserving my life until this day. Thank You for forgiving me. Thank You for sending Jesus to be our savior and Lord. Thank You for sending the Spirit to guide us. Thank You for the Bible, Your holy Word. Thank You for the church, my spiritual family. Thank You for my home and for my family. Thank You for my nation with its freedoms and its prosperity.* It is not difficult to give thanks to God.

Fourth, in their prayers Christians confess their sins to God and ask for forgiveness.

Fifth and finally, Christians offer their lives in commitment to God. This is a distinctive and important form of prayer, and it is quite easy to pray: *Father, so often in the past I have committed my life to You, and today I reaffirm my desire to be Your child and, with Your help, to live a life that will please You, my heavenly Father.*

When Christians follow the spirit of Jesus' instructions to pray "Our Father," they engage in a practice of immense richness and meaning, just as children who talk to their loving parents engage in a practice of great meaning and richness.

THE LIVES OF CHILDREN

So far we have seen that, because Christians are children of God, they should have a humble dependence on the Father, they should strive for childlike innocence and goodness, and they should talk simply and sincerely to their Father. Those things are all taught explicitly in the New Testament. It is possible for us to use our imaginations to identify other characteristics of children that are desirable for Christians. Four occur to me; they are playfulness, enthusiasm, wonder, and sincerity.

Play is so much a part of the lives of children that it is easy to overlook its profound meaning. When children play they create a world that is different from the world in which they live, one in which things are the way they're supposed to be, and in which pain and sadness and death do not occur. In doing this they show themselves to be sensitive spiritually to the possibility of a world that is better than our fallen one. One Christian writer, Peter Berger, has argued that the human propensity for play is a subtle hint of the reality of God.[5]

Enthusiasm is another quality that occurs naturally in the lives of healthy children. Children are capable of devoting themselves totally to a project or a person they love. As they grow older they learn to restrain their enthusiasms. It is necessary for them to do that, but it is unfortunate if they do it so thoroughly that in fact they no longer have the capacity for enthusiasm they had as children.

Wonder is also found in all healthy children. Since

children arrive in the world with no previous knowledge of the world, they are seeing everything for the first time, and it is all wonderful to them. With no false sense of dignity to maintain, they express the wonder they feel.

Sincerity also comes naturally to children. Their responses to things around them are unguarded and unreserved and therefore authentic. Christians need to work to maintain in their lives the kind of sincerity that comes so naturally to children.

CHILDLIKENESS AND CHILDISHNESS

From the lives of children we have chosen attitudes and practices that should characterize the lives of the children of God. It would, of course, be possible to identify attitudes in children's lives that should not characterize the lives of Christians. For example, children sometimes resist growing up. They prefer the security of remaining immature. Sometimes known as the Peter Pan Syndrome, this impulse is understandable, but it is not healthy, and it is not a model for Christians.

We need, therefore, to distinguish between the childlike qualities Christians should embrace and the childish qualities they should avoid. Another way to put this is to say that God's purpose is for Christians to grow into maturity.

Among human beings who live long enough, it sometimes happens that children and parents reverse roles. Elderly parents may become frail and dependent upon the children who once were weak and depended upon them. That does not happen with Christians, for God never becomes frail or dependent.

However, God's children do grow up, and they should. Peter urged his readers to grow in grace and in their knowledge of Christ (2 Peter 3:18) and to drink spiritual milk so that they would grow into salvation (1 Peter 2:2). Paul urged the Ephesians to speak the truth in love so that they would grow up to be like Christ; he even said that in that sense they were no longer to be like children (Ephesians 4:14–15). Just as good parents want their children to grow into mature adults, so God wants Christians to grow into mature Christians.

Adults always remain the children of their parents, and Christians who become spiritually mature retain their filial relationship to God as their Father. The difference is that they now relate to God as adult children rather than as young children. I think God is pleased when His children become mature adult children.

THE CHURCH AS FAMILY

As we have studied these images, we have noticed again and again how important the relationship with other Christians is. The image of child makes this especially clear. Since God is the Father of all Christians, then all Christians are brothers and sisters in the family of God. Jesus is their elder brother.

This means that, when Christians dislike each other or

quarrel with each other, they are disliking and quarreling with their own family members. We all know that family fights can be vicious, and that is true of fights between Christians. What makes it difficult to have peace in the Christian family is that Christians are so diverse. They all share many beliefs in common, but they also hold beliefs that differ from one another. They share many practices in common, but they also engage in practices that differ from one another.

How can they negotiate the differences? One option is to separate from each other; while this may be better than continual conflict, it also is not appropriate family behavior.

There is only one alternative to continual conflict or separation. It is the way of tolerance and forgiveness: "Be tolerant with one another and forgive one another whenever any of you has a complaint against someone else" (Colossians 3:13 TEV).

Tolerance does not have a good reputation among some Christ followers today. They assume that to be tolerant means either that you have no convictions or, if you have convictions, that you are quick to compromise them. In fact, tolerance is not compromise at all; tolerance is holding convictions deeply while maintaining peaceable relationships with people who do not share your convictions.

Forgiveness is also misunderstood. As we saw in chapter 2, forgiveness means we refuse to act on our natural impulse to take revenge on those who hurt us; instead, we live through the pain they have caused us, and the frustration we feel at not retaliating, until we come to the place where we no longer wish them ill but rather wish them well.

Tolerance and forgiveness make it possible for Christians who have different beliefs and practices, and who also have shortcomings, to live together peaceably in the family of God. All of us, without exception, need to incorporate into the way we live tolerance for the differences between ourselves and our sisters and brothers in the family of God, and forgiveness for our sisters and brothers. I share the conviction of Richard Mouw that we can "hold strongly felt convictions while still nurturing a spirit that is authentically kind and gentle."[6]

CONCLUSION

Christians are the children of God, born from above and intentionally adopted into the family of God. The lives of Christians, like the lives of children, should exhibit a humble dependence upon God and a childlike innocence. Throughout their lives, Christians should speak to God in prayer with the openness and sincerity that characterize the speech of children whose loving parents listen to them and are responsive to them. Christians' lives are enriched when they retain childlike qualities such as playfulness, wonder, enthusiasm, and sincerity. God's children should not remain infantile but grow up into mature persons, able to relate to their brothers and sisters in the family of God with tolerance and forgiveness.

CHAPTER 9

"I have called you friends."

—Jesus, in John 15:15

friend

It is easier for us to think of Jesus as our friend than it is for us to think of ourselves as Jesus' friends. We feel comfortable singing "What a Friend We Have in Jesus," but we might hesitate if we were asked to sing "What Good Friends We Are to Jesus." I think we can learn to think of ourselves as friends of Jesus, and we can learn what it takes to be good friends of Jesus.

It has been observed that persons who share romantic love talk continually of their love, but persons who share friendship rarely mention their friendship. Perhaps that helps us to understand why the Bible doesn't say a lot about friendship directly.

What we do find in the Bible are several stories of friends and their friendships. Perhaps the most famous friendship in the Bible is between Jonathan and David (see 1 Samuel 18:1–4, 19:1–7, 20:1–42). In Acts there is a story about some friends of Paul who intervene to protect him from a mob (Acts 19:31) and another story about an official who out of *philanthropia* (friendship) permitted Paul to get help from some friends (Acts 27:3). Occasionally Christians in the New Testament era referred to one another as friends (see 3 John 15), and today there is a church that calls itself the Society of Friends (Quakers).

FRIENDS OF GOD

In the Old Testament only two men are said to have been friends of God, namely, Abraham and Moses. The prophet Isaiah recorded this message from the Lord: "But you, Israel, my servant, Jacob, whom I have chosen, the offspring of Abraham, my friend…do not fear, for I am with you" (Isaiah 41:8–10), and in his epistle James wrote, "Abraham…was called the friend of God" (James 2:23).

In Exodus are stories about Moses going outside the camp from time to time in order to seek God's guidance, and when he did, "The LORD used to speak to Moses face to face, as one speaks to a friend" (Exodus 33:11).

The idea that God has friends is confirmed in two parables Jesus told about God's care for the lost. In the parables the people who represented God—a shepherd who lost his sheep and a woman who lost her coin—rejoiced with their friends when they found what they had lost (Luke 15:6, 9).

FRIENDS OF JESUS

The New Testament teaches that Jesus had friends. He was criticized for being a "friend of sinners" (Matthew 11:19), which, of course, He was. He spoke of Lazarus as His friend (John 11:11). John the Baptist spoke of himself as Jesus' friend (John 3:29).

The classic passage about Jesus' friends is John 15:12–15:

This is my commandment, that you love one another as I have loved you. No one has greater love than this, to lay down one's life for one's friends. You are my friends if you do what I command you. I do not call you servants any longer, because the servant does not know what the master is doing; but I have called you friends, because I have made known to you everything that I have heard from my Father.

As we read this passage we are struck by Jesus' contrast of the image of friend and the image of servant; Jesus says He now thinks of His followers as friends rather than as servants. In the second chapter of this book we saw how valuable the image of servant is—do these words of Jesus require us to set aside the image of servant?

I don't think so, and the simplest way to explain why is

to describe a problem that arises when we think of ourselves as friends of God or friends of Jesus. The problem has to do with what theologians call the transcendence of God. God is the absolute Lord of the universe, the one who created the universe out of nothing and who transcends the universe.

About a century ago a German theologian named Rudolf Otto wrote a book entitled *The Idea of the Holy*. In it he said that there is a primal, pre-rational experience that underlies all religion. His word for this experience was *numinous*, and he used a Latin phrase to describe its object, *mysterium tremendum et fascinans*, the Mystery that both frightens us and attracts us. The writers of the Bible were fully aware of God's utter transcendence, and they were reluctant to write anything that would undermine that truth about God.

The idea that God has human friends seems to do that. Friendship is ordinarily between people who are more or less equals, and the deeper the friendship, the more equal they become. But human beings are not equals of the transcendent God, so how can they experience friendship with God?

The answer is that this is a friendship between persons who are intrinsically unequal, and it has been made possible because the greater partner has condescended to befriend the lesser partner. The prophet Isaiah presented God's transcendence along with God's intention to enter into personal relationships with human beings when he recorded these words of God: "I am the high and holy God, who lives forever. I live in a high and holy place, but I also live with people who are humble and repentant, so that I can restore their confidence and hope" (Isaiah 57:15 TEV).

In the classic passage in John, Jesus expresses the same asymmetry by saying that His followers are His friends if they do what He commands. John would never have turned that around and said that Jesus will be our friend if He does what we command. Of course, Jesus has served us by saving us, but that is not the same thing as saying that He does what we command.

So, we have an asymmetrical friendship with Jesus, and with God, not as their equals, but with God as one who transcends us but condescends to us. And we have an asymmetrical friendship with Jesus as one who gives us commands, but has served us by sacrificing Himself for us. God's transcendence is clearer when we think of ourselves as God's servants than when we think of ourselves as God's friends, so we retain the image of servant as a way of reminding ourselves of God's transcendence.

Let us now consider some of the special things the image of friendship says to us.

FRIENDSHIP AND FREEDOM

Our friendship with Jesus is something into which we have voluntarily entered. Friendship is a relationship that is chosen, not thrust upon us. All of us were born into this world without our consent, but we have voluntarily entered into whatever friendships we have with others. It takes two people to make a friendship. One of the difficult lessons we have to learn during our adolescent years is that you cannot force an unwilling person to become your friend.

Usually friendships develop when one person takes the initiative and the other person responds, and that is true of our friendship with Jesus. Jesus told His followers, "You did not choose me but I chose you" (John 15:16). Jesus took the initiative to befriend us. Those who seek God and find God eventually learn that their seeking and finding were possible because God was first seeking and finding them. The most beautiful expression of this truth that I know of is found in the *Confessions* of St. Augustine, written about 400 A.D. Augustine prayed to God:

Late have I loved you, beauty so old and so new: late have I loved you. And see, you were within and I was in the external world and sought you there, and in my unlovely state I plunged into those lovely created things which you made. You were with me, and I was not with you. The lovely things kept me far from you, though if they did not have their existence in you, they had no existence at all. You called and cried out loud and shattered my deafness. You were radiant and resplendent, you put to flight my blindness. You were fragrant, and I drew in my breath and now pant after you. I tasted you, and I feel but hunger and thirst for you. You touched me, and I am set on fire to attain the peace which is yours.[1]

Jesus took the initiative to become our friend by providing the salvation we need and by offering to be our friend, and we have responded by trusting Him to be our savior and Lord, and our friend.

THE CLOSENESS OF FRIENDS

"There is a friend that sticketh closer than a brother" (Proverbs 18:24 KJV); we believe that is true of our friend Jesus. One of the ways friends come to be close to each other is by talking about their deepest concerns: "People with deep and lasting friendships…have a certain transparency, allowing people to see what is in their hearts."[2] We see this kind of transparency in Jesus' statement, "I have called you friends, because I have made known to you everything that I have heard from my Father" (John 15:15). The most important thing in Jesus' life was to know and serve His Father, and by sharing His Father's concerns with His followers, Jesus was establishing a close friendship with them. We know what concerns Jesus most deeply because He, our friend, has told us.

It is important that we reciprocate by talking to Jesus about what concerns us most deeply. We do this in prayer, of course, and that is why we treasure extemporaneous prayer so highly. While we welcome the guidance for prayer that we find in liturgies and written prayers such as the Psalms, we also keep a place in our private prayers for speaking to the Lord spontaneously, as a friend talks to a friend. We can be absolutely transparent with Jesus; we do

189

not need to attempt to conceal anything from Him, not even the darkest and most unpleasant parts of our lives. He has told us what is most important to Him; we should tell Him what is most important to us.

There is a paradox about friendship, namely, that as friends become transparent with each other, each learns that there is a mystery about the other and both learn that there is a mystery about friendship itself. "The chemistry of friendship...is a mystery."[3] That is true of our friendship with Jesus. We do not understand it fully, and we do not understand Jesus fully. While we know that Jesus' deepest concern was that people love God with all their hearts and their neighbors as themselves (Matthew 22:24–30), it never occurs to us that we understand everything there is to know about Jesus. A mystery remains—the mystery of why God, who had no need for a world, created a world with human beings and showered love upon us and even acted sacrificially in Jesus to befriend us in spite of our sin.

In the New Testament there is a word for the closeness of friendship that Christians have with the Lord; it is the word *koinonia*, and it refers to shared life and usually is translated *fellowship*. For example, John said that he wrote his letter "so that you also may have fellowship with us; and truly our fellowship is with the Father and with his Son Jesus Christ. We are writing these things so that our joy may be complete" (1 John 1:3–4).

The connection between friendship and joy that John mentions is not accidental. It is characteristic of friends that they rejoice in each other's existence. Friends are glad their friends are alive and present with them.

We believe that God our friend rejoices in our existence; in fact, we believe that if God didn't rejoice in our existence, we would not exist, since it is God who gives us our existence. Once you believe that God rejoices in your existence, you naturally will feel gratitude to God and trust in God. To put the same thing the other way around, people who do not feel gratitude to God and trust in God probably have failed to grasp the fact that God is really happy that they exist.

And we who are Jesus' friends are happy about Jesus' existence. We are glad that He has come into our world, and we are glad that He has taken the initiative to befriend us. We would not have it any other way. The connection between friendship and joy is very strong.

FRIENDS CARE FOR EACH OTHER

The connection between friendship and caring is strong, too. It would be self-contradictory to say, "I am your friend, but I do not care whether you are happy or unhappy, well or ill, flourishing or suffering." Friends care for each other and wish each other well.

We believe that God cares deeply for us. We are "convinced that neither death, nor life, nor angels, nor rulers, nor things present, nor things to come, nor powers, nor height, nor depth, nor anything else in all creation, will be able to separate us from the love of God in Christ Jesus our

Lord" (Romans 8:38–39). God's love for us is an affection that God feels, but it also is an action that God takes: "We know love by this, that he laid down his life for us" (1 John 3:16).

And we reciprocate: "We love because he first loved us" (1 John 4:19). We care about Jesus personally. We don't just believe things about Jesus; we believe in Jesus. We don't just think about Jesus; we love Jesus. We don't just know about Jesus, we know Jesus, personally. We care about Him.

We also care about the things He cared about. One of my friends, Walter Shurden, has described his work as a university professor this way: "I am trying to get my students to take seriously what Jesus took seriously." It's difficult to think of a more important enterprise, or a more needed one.

There is a form of Christian faith that has emphasized the closeness of the caring relationship between Christians and Christ; it is called pietism. There is a tendency in pietism to say that, unless you have a close personal relationship such as this, you cannot be a really good Christian at all.

I see the point of this, and in a general way I am supportive. Yet there are people who are sincere in their Christian faith and for whom the center of gravity in their faith is not their close personal relationship with the Lord.

For example, for some Christians the center of gravity in their faith and life is their worship of God. They believe that nothing is more important than for Christians to gather together and to "worship the LORD in the beauty of holiness" (Psalm 96:9 KJV).

For other Christians the center of gravity in their lives is working for peace and justice in the world. These people are the heirs of the prophets of the Old Testament, who said things such as, "Let justice roll down like waters, and righteousness like an ever-flowing stream" (Amos 5:24). They also are the heirs of Jesus, who said, "Blessed are the peacemakers, for they will be called children of God" (Matthew 5:9).

For still other Christians the center of gravity of faith is found in evangelism and missions. There are entire denominations whose principal (or even sole) reason for existing is to do this important work. For example, when the Southern Baptist Convention was organized in 1845, the founders issued a statement describing their new enterprise as "a plan for eliciting, combining, and directing the energies of the whole denomination in one sacred effort, for the propagation of the Gospel."[4]

I think that most of us would respond to these observations by saying, "Why can't we do all these things? Why can't we be seriously committed to a close personal friendship with the Lord *and* to worship *and* to peace and justice *and* to evangelism and missions?"

The answer, of course, is that we can. Both in our personal lives and in our churches, we can commit ourselves to all these things, and we should. Nevertheless, it does turn out that, in fact, many Christians tend to make one or the other of these things the center of gravity in their Christian faith.

I do not think this has to be a problem. My justification for this is Paul's insistence that different Christians have different gifts (1 Corinthians 12). It seems inevitable that, with our different gifts (not to mention our different histories and cultures), different Christians are going to find the center of gravity in our faith at different places.

FRIENDS ARE LOYAL

If friendships last very long, they probably will be tested. Tests can come from outside, but usually they come from within. Because we put so much trust in our friends, we are particularly vulnerable to the way they treat us; if they are not perfectly loyal to us, or even if we do not feel that they are perfectly loyal to us, we can be deeply hurt, and that damages our friendship and may put it at risk.

Jesus is a loyal friend, and He never does anything to betray His friendship with us. Nevertheless, Christians sometimes feel that Jesus has not been good to them. Frequently this feeling is the product of a false assumption.

Many Christians have assumed that since God has saved them they will not have to experience the suffering that other people in the world experience. Those who make this assumption and then experience suffering easily become disappointed with God; they feel that God has let them down—not been a good friend to them.

194

The problem lies, of course, in the assumption itself, but it is not always easy to see that, especially when you are suffering deeply. Therefore it is a good idea for us, during times when we are not suffering, to intentionally identify and then abandon the mistaken assumption. We will be helped to do this if we remember that, just a few hours after He said the words, "You are my friends," our friend Jesus Himself was suffering terribly. There is joy in friend-ship, and God does protect and bless His friends, but God does not shield us from all suffering any more than He shielded Jesus from all suffering.

Many Christians who have felt disappointment at the sufferings they have experienced have nevertheless remained loyal to God. This is a wonderful thing, for loy-alty is one of the most important qualities of friends. Friends are loyal to each other in ways they can't explain. Sometimes, when someone says, "You shouldn't continue to be her friend; look at what she did," we may not be able to offer a coherent account of why we are going to continue to be her friend; but we are going to do so, because we know that, despite what has been suggested, she really is our friend.

So it is with our friend Jesus. Others may not under-stand why we do not discontinue our friendship with Him, given our suffering or whatever, but we intend to remain loyal to Him for reasons we find difficult, or even impossi-ble, to explain.

An early Christian leader named Polycarp who lived in

what is now Turkey offered a moving account of his loyalty to Christ under difficult circumstances. He was born about 25 years after Jesus was crucified, and apparently he was personally acquainted with the apostle John. In the middle of the second century he was condemned to be executed because of his faith, but he was told that his life would be spared if he transferred his loyalty from Christ to Caesar. Polycarp replied, "For eighty-six years I have been his servant, and he has done me no wrong. How can I blaspheme my King who saved me?"[5] That is one of the clearest accounts of loyalty to Christ I know of. Polycarp was loyal to the end, and he paid for his loyalty with his life.

Christians believe that Jesus is completely loyal to them, and they know that they should be loyal to Him in response. Of course, they also know, in their more lucid moments, that sometimes they are disloyal to Jesus.

Disloyalty doesn't usually take a dramatic form such as betraying Christ publicly the way Polycarp was urged to do. The forms of disloyalty to Jesus are usually subtle rather than dramatic. Loyalty to Jesus consists of obeying His command, and His command consists of one thing: "This is my commandment, that you love one another" (John 15:12). Lovelessness in any form is disloyalty to Jesus, whether it is selfishness, laziness, or indifference to the pain of others.

THE COMMUNITY OF FRIENDS

Christians are not only friends of Jesus; they also are friends to each other. One way to think of the church is as a community of people who are learning to be friends to each other.

Some Christians belong to congregations that are so large that it isn't possible to learn every member's name, let along become friends in a meaningful sense with everyone. Near my home there is a church so large that it would take seven weeks of round-the-clock visiting to spend just ten minutes with each of the members. What happens ideally in a church like that is two things. First, the members of the congregation maintain a friendly attitude to each other, wishing them well, being loyal to each other. Second, the members develop friendships in a more meaningful sense with a small group within the congregation.

Some people are better at cultivating friendships than others, but all of us can learn to do it, and ministers can learn to build community within their congregations. It's important to do this. The church members in Jerusalem devoted themselves to fellowship (Acts 2:42), and so must we.

If you ask people why they continue to be active in the life of their churches, there is a good chance they will tell you, "Because my friends are there." People love their churches because of the music, because of the preaching and teaching, and because of the good programs for their children, but for many Christians it is the ties of friendship that they treasure most.

Friendships must be entered into voluntarily; ministers can't make them happen. What churches can do is to affirm the importance of friendships and then build into the church's programming times and opportunities for friendships to develop. There is something odd about telling people to stop visiting with each other so they can have a Bible study on fellowship.

CONCLUSION

Our human need for friends is very deep. God addresses that need by befriending us in Jesus and also by creating the church to be a community of friends on earth.

CHAPTER 10

"I will dwell in the house of the LORD for ever."

—Psalm 23:6 KJV

Guest

"Practice hospitality," the apostle Paul instructed the church in Rome (Romans 12:13 REB), and it is good counsel for Christians today.

Practicing hospitality is a way of expressing love. For Christians love includes emotions: we rejoice in those we love, we feel affection for them, and we care about them and wish them well. But love is not just emotion; it is also action. One of the ways to express your love for others is to offer them hospitality. We love people by welcoming them as guests in our homes.

We may invite people to be our guests for a meal or at a special party. We may have overnight guests, or guests who stay for a longer visit.

Hospitality was highly prized in the ancient Near East, and it certainly was appropriate for Christians to carry on the tradition of hospitality. The writer of Hebrews reminded his readers that sometimes, when we show hospitality to strangers, we may be entertaining angels (Hebrews 13:1–2); perhaps he was thinking about the time when Sarah and Abraham welcomed three men as guests, only to discover later that the men were angels who brought them a message from God (Genesis 18:1–22).

THE HOUSE OF GOD

We are interested now in how we as Christians are guests of the hospitality of God. But does God have a house into which to welcome guests?

In one sense, of course, God does not have a house. Theologians say that God is omnipresent, that is, present in all places at all times without being confined to any one place. Psalm 139 tells us that God is present everywhere.

Yet the Bible also speaks of God as having a house. The first house of God was the tabernacle, a moveable tent that the then-nomadic Israelites took with them as they traveled. Then, in the tenth century before Christ, King Solomon built in Jerusalem a Temple to be a permanent house of God. Solomon was perfectly aware that the Temple did not confine God, for at its dedication he prayed,

"Even heaven and the highest heaven cannot contain you, much less this house that I have built!" (1 Kings 8:27). He asked only that God would be present in the Temple.

And God was. "The LORD is in his holy Temple," the psalmist prayed (Psalm 11:4). Devout people in Israel came to love being in Jerusalem in the house of the Lord. We see this, for example, in Psalm 84, which is a celebration of the Temple:

How lovely is your dwelling place, O LORD of hosts! My soul longs, indeed it faints for the courts of the LORD.... Happy are those who live in your house, ever singing your praise.... For a day in your courts is better than a thousand elsewhere. I would rather be a doorkeeper in the house of my God than live in the tents of wickedness.

—Psalm 84:1–10

All people were invited to God's house. While it is natural to think of the Temple as a place for Jews to worship God, in fact the prophet Isaiah reported that the Lord had said, "My house shall be called a house of prayer for all peoples" (Isaiah 56:7). God offered hospitality to all people.

JESUS AND THE TEMPLE

By the time Jesus came on the scene, the Temple Solomon had built had been destroyed and rebuilt twice. When Jesus was twelve years old He went with His family to the Temple, and He spoke of the Temple as "my Father's

201

house" (Luke 2:49). As an adult Jesus apparently did not go often to the Temple; most of His public ministry took place in Galilee, which was a considerable distance from Jerusalem and the Temple. He did go to the Temple occasionally, however.

Jesus spent the last week of His life on earth in and near Jerusalem, and while He was there He did something that was very unusual for Him. He used physical force to drive from the Temple some of the merchants who had been conducting their business there (Matthew 21:12–17, Mark 11:15–18, Luke 19:45–48). This is a difficult story for me, and let me tell you why.

What most appeals to me about Jesus is His grace toward all people, His kindness, His generosity, His acceptance of unacceptable people, and His patience. But that is not the side of His personality that we see on this Monday of the last week before His crucifixion. What we see instead is His anger. He was so angry about what was going on in the Temple that He physically drove the merchants and bankers out of the Temple.

This makes me very uneasy. It has implications for my life. If Jesus became angry with those people long ago, might He become angry with me? Therefore, it is very important to know exactly why Jesus got angry. What does this anger of Jesus mean?

Does it mean that He was opposed to all the religious rituals of the Temple? No, that can't be the case, because at other times Jesus spoke with approval of one who gave money to support the work of the Temple (see Luke 21:1–4).

Does Jesus' anger mean simply that He did not like religious people, that He thought that people who carefully observe religious practices are somehow bound to miss the point of it all? No, that can't be the case either, because at other times He spoke with approval of people who prayed and fasted and attended worship services. In fact, He Himself seems regularly to have attended worship in synagogues on Sabbath days and at times to have participated in them.

So I am left with a question: Why was Jesus so angry? As I have studied these passages, I have come to believe that two things made Jesus angry.

First, He was angry that the Temple was being misused. It was supposed to be a house of prayer, or, as we would say today, a place set aside for the worship of God. Instead, it was being used for other purposes. We have to read between the lines to discover what the other purposes were. There may have been excessive business enterprises. Two kinds of business were being transacted in the Temple. First, merchants were selling animals and birds to the pilgrims. The pilgrims gave these to the priests to be sacrificed. It was much easier for pilgrims to buy these animals when they arrived in Jerusalem than to bring them with them on what was, for some of them, a long and difficult journey. Selling doves in the Temple was a useful practice and an honorable way to make a living.

Then there were the bankers. They exchanged the money that the pilgrims brought with them for silver coins minted in the city of Tyre; these latter coins were the only kind which were acceptable for paying the Temple tax, which provided money that supported the work of the Temple. This too was a useful practice, and an honorable way to make a living.

It is possible that Jesus was angry simply because the people involved in the commerce had become too greedy. But we don't have any evidence that this was the case.

A second possibility is that the merchants and bankers were being dishonest and cheating the pilgrims, many of whom may have been poor people. We do not have any direct evidence that this was going on. However, Jesus does refer to a "den of thieves," and He may have meant that the bankers and merchants were cheating the pilgrims.

There is a third possibility. The phrase "den of thieves" may refer simply to a gathering place for evil people of all kinds. If this is the case, Jesus may have been referring, not to the bankers and merchants, but to other people who were meeting in the Temple area to make evil plans. It is possible that their evil plans were political in nature. That is, people were meeting in the Temple to plot insurrection against the Romans. Remember, Israel was an occupied territory. The Temple would be an ideal place for revolutionaries to meet, because not many Romans would be there, and there were inner courts into which the Romans could not go.

What is the point here? It is that God has given His people a great privilege. He has come to live in their midst, in the Temple, "The House of the Lord." God expected His people to remember that His presence among them is a privilege, and to act accordingly.

Instead, they were neglecting His presence in favor of one or more of these other practices: making a living by banking and by selling doves, or cheating poor pilgrims, or plotting revolution against the Romans.

It was, I think, the fact that they were taking God's presence for granted that made Jesus angry.

We are all familiar with what it means to neglect someone. It is a perennial human temptation. A husband simply begins to presume upon his wife's love; a wife simply begins to take her husband for granted. Unfortunately, it happens all the time. In order for a marriage to be strong, spouses must never take each other for granted but rather be intentionally caring, sensitive, and interested in each other. So it is in our relationship with God. We must never take God for granted. We must not forget the grace and love and kindness of God to us.

I think something else made Jesus angry too. It was what was happening in the outer court, the court of the Gentiles. To appreciate this, it helps if we understand the layout of the Temple. The Temple area was enormous, about 35 acres. That's several city blocks. Around the sides of this great area King Herod had built enormous porches with large columns. In these porches were the merchants and the bankers.

Most of the vast Temple area was called the Court of the Gentiles, and it was open to everyone. As we have seen, the prophet Isaiah had written (56:1–8) that the Lord intended that people from all nations should come to His Temple to worship Him. And some Gentiles certainly wanted to worship the God of Israel. They were attracted to Israel's God by the conviction of the Israelites that there is one and only one true and living God. They also were attracted by the high moral standards of the Hebrew religion in contrast to the often deplorably low moral standards of other religions.

So the Gentiles came to the Temple to worship God, and God welcomed the Gentiles into His house.

All of the Temple was a holy place, a place for worship. This was as true of the great outer area into which the Gentiles could go as it was of the inner areas that were reserved for Jews. So, for example, the Mishnah, a collection of sayings of the rabbis, says that no one should walk across the Temple mount as a shortcut. You were to come here to worship, not to use it as a thoroughfare.

Near the center of the great area, there was a smaller area in the shape of a rectangle enclosed with a wall about 3 feet high. On that low wall signs were posted which said that any Gentile found within this wall would be put to death. Some of those signs have been found by archaeologists.

Jews walked from the great outer court into this smaller area, usually through a gate at the east end of the rectangle called "The Beautiful Gate." They were then in the court of the women—Jewish women only, of course.

The Jewish men could continue farther into the rectangle, up some stairs and through a gate called the Nicanor or East Gate. They then had to stop in a relatively small area called the Court of the Israelites.

From this court they could see into the inner part of the Temple, called the Court of the Priests. At the center of the Court of the Priests there stood the Temple itself. It was a rectangular building, tall and narrow. When King Herod had rebuilt it, he had covered it with gold. Only the priests went into the area around the Temple itself and into the Temple itself.

Inside this Temple building there were two rooms. The first was a large room into which all the priests could go at any time. The smaller, inner room was called the Holy of Holies. Only the High Priest went into it, and only one day a year, on the Day of Atonement, called *Yom Kippur*.

As you can see, everything about the Temple area spoke of the special status of certain groups of people. The Gentiles were restricted to the larger Temple mount area. The Jewish women were restricted to a court where they could not see the Temple proper. The Jewish men who were not priests were restricted to a court from which they could observe but not participate in the most sacred acts of worship.

That is a bad system, isn't it? It's a class system. Except for the Holy of Holies, it was not a system prescribed by the Old Testament. It was a system that grew up across the centuries. Presumably it was all done to help the people feel reverence for God and respect for the holy.

However, it was not this system of restricting people that made Jesus so angry that Monday. Perhaps He did not like it, but that is not what made Him angry. What made Him angry was that the people did not even follow that system, bad as it was. Instead, they treated the great outer area, the court of the Gentiles, with complete contempt.

It was bad enough that the Gentiles were excluded from the most important acts of worship. But some of the Jews did not settle for that. They looked with contempt upon the court of the Gentiles. They felt free to interrupt the Gentiles who came to that court to worship God. They walked through that court carrying vessels. They used that court to sell doves, and to exchange money. I think this is what made Jesus so angry: the contempt for the Gentiles who attempted to worship God in the Temple.

The more I think about it, the more I understand why Jesus became angry. Could there be anything more insensitive than to take God for granted, or more cruel than to look with contempt upon some group of people who are attempting to worship God?

And so I have asked myself, are you taking God for granted? Are you presuming upon God's goodness and then going on to things that you think are more important than God, things such as having a comfortable life? Are you neglecting God, even as you go about your work as a minister?

And I also ask myself, are there people upon whom you feel entitled to look with total contempt? Do you feel contempt for people of a different race? Do you feel contempt for your students who are not good students? Do you feel contempt for liberals, or for fundamentalists? Is there a group of people you can speak of with a sneer—and feel good about doing it?

As I asked myself these questions, I discovered something that surprised me.

I discovered that I am glad that Jesus got angry about these things. I am glad that Jesus got angry when people neglected God, and I'm glad He got angry when people looked with contempt upon other human beings. After all, what is the alternative to His getting angry?

The historian Edward Gibbon once wrote, "The various modes of worship, which prevailed in the Roman world, were all considered by the people as equally true; by the philosopher, as equally false; and by the magistrate, as equally useful."[1]

I am glad that Jesus did not hold any of those opinions. He did not say that all religions are equally true, and He did not say that all are equally false. And He did not say all are to be used for political enterprises such as keeping people docile.

Jesus knew that the truth is that there is one and only

one living God and that this God cares for all people. By becoming angry with people who took that God for granted and who looked with contempt upon those who were not born into God's covenant people, Jesus acted in the best interests of us all. If He had let these things pass, He would not have been our friend. If He cared enough to condemn these practices, He cared enough to save us from them. We need to be saved from taking God for granted, and we need to be saved from looking with contempt upon any people.

So it turns out that, when Jesus got angry that day, He did us a favor. He alerted us to two things that we must at all costs avoid in our lives. We must never presume upon God, and we must never look with contempt upon any people.

Jesus felt that God invited all people to be guests in the Temple, and that God extended hospitality to everyone who would come to the Temple with the sincere desire to worship God.

JESUS AND THE HOSPITALITY OF GOD

Near the end of His life on earth Jesus told a parable about God's hospitality to guests (Matthew 22:1–14). It was about a king who invited people to come to a wedding banquet for his son. The king represented God, and the son represented Jesus Himself. The king told his servants to go out into the streets and extend his invitation to people "both good and bad" to come to the banquet.

210

With this parable the idea of God's hospitality shifts away from the physical Temple in Jerusalem; God is pictured in the parable as inviting all kinds of people to a wedding banquet in a place that transcends the Temple. In fact, on one occasion Jesus predicted that a time was coming when the Temple would be destroyed (Luke 21:5–6), a prediction that was fulfilled in A.D. 70 when the Romans destroyed the Temple. In thinking of God's hospitality apart from the Temple, Jesus was returning to the theme that Solomon had recognized and which theologians call God's omnipresence. He was thinking of a spiritual house of God, a spiritual Temple.

A SPIRITUAL TEMPLE

Peter spoke about a Temple in a spiritual sense; he believed that the Christian church is a Temple in which God lives on earth, and that every church member is a brick in the Temple: "Like living stones, let yourselves be build into a spiritual house" (1 Peter 2:5). Paul taught the same thing and said that Jesus is the cornerstone of the building: "You are…built…with Christ Jesus himself as the cornerstone. In him the whole structure is joined together and grows into a holy temple in the Lord" (Ephesians 2:19–21).

Here I am mixing the metaphors a little. Every Christian is a stone in the house of the Lord, but every Christian also is a guest in the house of the Lord.

Despite the mixed metaphors, the point that Peter and

Paul were making is clear: as we participate in the life of the church—its witness, its fellowship, its worship of God—we are guests of God in the house of God.

One of the principal components of Christian worship gives us an especially vivid understanding of ourselves as God's guests. I am speaking of communion. As we eat bread and drink wine at the Lord's table, we experience God's hospitality. Communion has many levels of meaning; one of them is that we are the Lord's guests. I believe that Jesus desires to share this symbolic meal with us just as He desired to share the last supper with His disciples in Jerusalem (see Luke 22:15). At His table, we who are His guests experienced the hospitality of Jesus our host.

PRIVILEGE AND RESPONSIBILITY

The image of Christians as guests has a lot in common with some of the other images we have reviewed, for example, that we are God's children and that we are friends of God. But one thing is different about our being guests. The other images call attention to particular duties we have—to be good children, to be good friends, and so on. The image of guest says almost nothing about our responsibilities; its emphasis falls almost entirely on our privileges.

As we near the end of this study of images for Christ followers, it is well to remind ourselves that, though God has given us serious responsibilities, God also has given us great privileges. It is a privilege to be disciples of Jesus, children of God, and so on. It is a very great privilege to be guests of God, invited by God to the wedding feast of the Son of God.

Do guests have any responsibilities? I suppose we are responsible to dress appropriately for the wedding (see Matthew 22:11–14), which presumably means to be aware that it was generous of God to invite us to this important event. In the words of the psalmist, we should "enter his gates with thanksgiving" (Psalm 100:4).

Mostly, though, we are simply to come and to enjoy God's hospitality. When we receive God's generous hospitality with gratitude, we will be the kind of guests God wants us to be.

Gratitude can be a way of life for God's guests. We can be thankful people, not just people who happen incidentally to express thanks from time to time. We can live in such a way that our lives become an extended *thank you* to God.

We are all routinely offered opportunities to live lives characterized by things other than gratitude. For example, we can live competitively rather than gratefully. We can commit ourselves to success above all other things.

Another way of life is the resentful life. We can devote our attention to what is wrong in life, especially to what is unfair about the way we ourselves are treated. We can surrender ourselves to cynicism about life, ignoring what is good and beautiful and honorable about it. We can descend into bitterness about life, even into contempt for life and the world and everything in it. In the resentful life there is no room for gratitude because there is no acknowledgment of what God has done for us.

Another way of life is an anxious life. In an anxious life we concentrate on the future and the troubles it may possibly bring to us or to those we love. As surprising as it may sound, some Christians actually live with anxiety and fear that God is going to get them. By *fear* I do not mean respect for God, which is a good thing; I mean terror that God may turn against them. In an anxious life we are too worried to be thankful.

Another way to live is a dutiful life. I certainly do not want to say anything negative about doing our duty in life, for that is a very honorable thing, as we saw in our study of the image of servant in chapter 2. But there is a kind of joyless dutifulness that is not the way we are called to live, and it is joyless because it lacks gratitude.

So a thankful life is an alternative to a competitive life, a resentful life, an anxious life, and a joylessly dutiful life. Lord Byron described the life of gratitude beautifully in "The Prayer of Nature":

To Thee I breathe my humble strain,
Grateful for all Thy mercies past,
And hope, my God, to Thee again
This erring life may fly at last.[2]

THE FINAL BANQUET

We have seen that there is a sense in which we are already guests of God, enjoying God's hospitality in the church, which is God's Temple, and experiencing God's generosity at the table of the Lord.

But there is another sense, which also is important, in which we look forward to a future time when we "will dwell in the house of the Lord for ever" (Psalm 23:6 KJV). While it can be difficult to face fully the fact of our mortality, at some level we are aware of the fact that we will not live on this earth forever. We also are aware of the fact that the only hope we have for a future life is in God; certainly there is nothing we can do to raise ourselves from the dead. The resurrection of Jesus has given us hope for our own resurrection.

But what shall we experience in the world to come? Will it be a god who is indifferent to us, or hostile to us, or threatening to us? No, indeed. What we will experience will be a God of generous, magnanimous hospitality who invites us to share in a great celebration. Here is how the prophet Isaiah expressed this hope:

Here on Mount Zion the LORD Almighty will prepare a banquet for all the nations of the world—a banquet of the richest food and the finest wine. Here he will suddenly remove the cloud of sorrow that has been hanging over all the nations. The Sovereign LORD will destroy death forever! He will wipe away the tears from everyone's eyes and take away the disgrace his people have suffered throughout the world. The LORD himself has spoken.

When it happens, everyone will say, "He is our God! We have put our trust in him, and he has rescued us. He is the

LORD! We have put our trust in him, and now we are happy and joyful because he has saved us."

—Isaiah 25:6–9 TEV

I believe this.

I believe that God is going to prepare a banquet for all the nations of the world.

I believe that God is going to remove all the sorrow from the world.

I believe that God is going to wipe away the tears from everyone's eyes.

I believe that God is going to take away the disgrace His people have suffered.

I believe that, when God does this, we will all honor God and say that we are happy because God has saved us.

It is going to be wonderful to be a guest at God's great banquet.

At the end of the second century, the bishop of Lyons in France, St. Irenaeus, wrote a long book defending traditional Christian faith and opposing many erroneous ideas about the faith. In the course of his book he wrote these words: *"Gloria enim Dei vivens homo,"* the glory of God is a human being who is fully alive.[1]

When I first read Irenaeus's statement, I thought he must have been mistaken. Surely, I thought, the glory of God is most evident in the creation of the vast and mysterious and beautiful cosmos; doesn't the Bible say that "the heavens declare the glory of God" (Psalm 19:1 KJV)?

But the more I reflected on it, the more I saw Irenaeus's point. God has created many things that display the divine glory; nothing displays God's glory more effectively than human beings, who are created in the image of God.

But God's glory is not visible in human beings when, like the fearful servant in Jesus' parable, they hide the gifts God has entrusted to them (see Matthew 25:14–30). It is when human beings live their lives fully, making use of all that God has given them in creation and redemption, that they most fully display the glory of God.

I have found that the images of Christ followers in the New Testament can help us to be fully alive as Christians and as human beings. They have helped me, and I hope they will help you who read this book, too.

Don't let the images become a burden to you. That's not

why we have them. They have been given to us to help us with our lives and our burdens, not to add to our burdens.

The best way to let them help you is to think about them reflectively. You can do this on the run—when you're driving, or when you're waiting for someone, or when you're working in your yard. Even better, you can set aside time to meditate on them.

If you are a visual person, you might try to visualize yourself as a member of the original group of Jesus' disciples, or as a guest at God's banquet, or as a friend of Jesus, and so on. In your reflections, be a participant, not an observer. Try to put yourself in the picture.

If you are a more verbal person, you might try reading slowly and reflectively the Scripture passages about the images.

I have included ideas about what we do because we're disciples, servants, and so on. See if you can think of additional things we are to do. What do you think disciples should do? Or soldiers? Or children of God? Doubtless you can think of other ways to make use of this Bible study.

May the Lord bless you as you study these images. I hope your study will be as meaningful an experience for you as mine has been for me.

Preface

1. Paul S. Minear, *Images of the Church in the New Testament* (Philadelphia: The Westminster Press, 1960, 1977), 21.

2. Margaret Miles, "Pilgrimage as Metaphor in a Nuclear Age," *Theology Today* 45:2 (July 1988): 166.

Introduction

1. Harriet Crabtree, *The Christian Life,* Harvard Dissertations in Religion 29 (Minneapolis: Fortress Press, 1991), xix. This doctoral dissertation is a sympathetic and insightful study of the use of biblical images for Christ followers in popular Protestant, Catholic, and Orthodox writing about Christian living during the second half of the twentieth century.

Chapter One

1. Lawrence Richards suggests that the idea of discipleship is rare in the New Testament because, after Jesus' departure, there was no one to whom Christians could submit as disciples submitted to their rabbis. See Lawrence O. Richards, "The Disappearing Disciple: Why Is the Use of 'Disciple' Limited to the Gospels and Acts?," *Evangelical Journal* 10:1 (Spring 1992): 3–11.

2. Dallas Willard, *The Divine Conspiracy: Rediscovering Our Hidden Life in God* (San Francisco: HarperSanFrancisco, 1998), xiii.

3. Dallas Willard, *The Divine Conspiracy: Rediscovering Our Hidden Life in God* (San Francisco: HarperSanFrancisco, 1998), 271, 273.

4. C.H. Dodd, *Gospel and Law* (New York: Columbia University Press, 1951, 1960), 41–42.

5. Albert Schweitzer, *The Quest of the Historical Jesus*, trans. W. Montgomery (New York: The Macmillan Company, 1961), 403.

6. Dietrich Bonhoeffer, *The Cost of Discipleship*, trans. R. H. Fuller (New York: The Macmillan Company, 1963), 43.

Chapter Two
1. Dale B. Martin, *Slavery as Salvation* (New Haven: Yale University Press, 1990), 147. Other scholars disagree with Martin; see, for example, John Byron, *Slavery Metaphors in Early Judaism and Pauline Christianity* (Tübingen: Mohr Siebeck, 2003), 7–12.

2. The poem is available at http://www.englishverse.com/poems/on_his_blindness.

3. Martin Luther, *Three Treatises*, trans. W. A. Lambert (Philadelphia: Fortress Press, 1960), 277–78.

4. Rajmohan Gandhi, "Gandhi's Unfulfilled Legacy: Prospects for Reconciliation in Racial/Ethnic Conflict," *Theology & Public Policy* 7:1 (Summer, 1995): 12.

Chapter Three
1. Douglas John Hall, *The Steward*, rev. ed. (Grand Rapids: William B. Eerdmans Publishing Company, 1990), 32.

2. Laura Smit, "The Image of Home," *Theology Today* 45:3 (October 1988): 308.

3. Albert C. Outler, ed., *John Wesley* (New York: Oxford University Press, 1964), 238–250.

4. In *The Baptist Hymnal* (Nashville: Convention Press, 1991), 267.

Chapter Four
1. Roland H. Bainton, *Christian Attitudes Toward War and Peace* (Nashville: Abingdon Press, 1960, 1982), 66–68.

2. Harriet Crabtree, *The Christian Life,* Harvard Dissertations in Religion 29 (Minneapolis: Fortress Press, 1991), 89.

3. Owen Chadwick, trans. and editor, *Western Asceticism* (Philadelphia: The Westminster Press, 1958), 62–63.

Chapter Five
1. Harriet Crabtree, *The Christian Life,* Harvard Dissertations in

Religion 29 (Minneapolis: Fortress Press, 1991), 16 (speaking of the work of Nathalie Bruyère-Demoulin).

2. Edward M. Hallowell, *Connect* (New York: Pocket Books, 1999), xii.

3. See Jay Weiner, "Do Nice Guys Finish...Blessed?" in the Minneapolis *Star Tribune* at www.startribune.com/viewers/story.php?template=print_a&story=484 9591.

4. Brother Lawrence, *The Practice of the Presence of God*, arranged and edited by Douglas V. Steere (Nashville: The Upper Room, 1950), 20, 9.

Chapter Six
1. Margaret Miles, "Pilgrimage as Metaphor in a Nuclear Age," *Theology Today* 45:2 (July 1988): 170.

2. Geddes MacGregor, *God Beyond Doubt: An Essay in the Philosophy of Religion* (Philadelphia: J. B. Lippincott Company, 1966), 86.

3. Stanley Hauerwas and William H. Willimon, *Resident Aliens: Life in the Christian Colony* (Nashville: Abingdon Press, 1989), 53.

4. Margaret Miles, "Pilgrimage as Metaphor in a Nuclear Age," *Theology Today* 45:2 (July 1988): 168.

5. J.B. Lightfoot and J.R. Harmer, editors and translators, *The Apostolic Fathers*, second edition (Grand Rapids: Baker Book House, 1992), 541–43; from *The Epistle to Diognetus*, 5–6.

6. St. Bernard of Clairvaux, *On Loving God*, is available on the web at the following address: www.ccel.org/ccel/bernard/loving_god.html. These ideas are found in chapters 8, 9, and 15.

7. *The Baptist Hymnal*, 208. Apparently Wesley borrowed the phrase from an earlier hymn by Joseph Addison entitled "When All Thy Mercies, O My God," *The Baptist Hymnal* (Nashville: Convention Press, 1975), 468. See J.R. Watson, *The English Hymn* (Oxford: Clarendon Press, 1997), 246.

8. Gilbert K. Chesterton, *Orthodoxy* (New York: John Lane Company, 1909), 14–19.

9. T.S. Eliot, "Four Quartets" at http://www.tristan.icom43.net/quartets/gidding.html.

10. From "God's Grandeur" by Gerard Manley Hopkins. It may be seen at http://www.poetryloverspage.com/utilities/wwwboard/messages/1487.html.

Chapter Seven
1. "Holy Eucharist, Rite I, The Prayers of the People" in The Book of Common Prayer (New York: The Church Hymnal Corporation, 1979), 329.

Chapter Eight
1. Article II, *The Baptist Faith and Message*, available at http://www.sbc.net/bfm/bfm2000.asp#ii.

2. Malcolm O. Tolbert, *Good News from Matthew* (Nashville: Broadman Press, 1955), 154.

3. Albert C. Outler, ed., *John Wesley* (New York: Oxford University Press, 1964), 258.

4. Henry van Dyke, "Joyful, Joyful, We Adore Thee," *The Baptist Hymnal* (Nashville: Convention Press, 1991), 7.

5. Peter Berger, *A Rumor of Angels* (Garden City: Anchor Books, 1969), 57–60.

6. Richard Mouw, *Uncommon Decency* (Downers Grove: InterVarsity Press, 1992), 15. This book is about tolerance without compromise.

Chapter Nine
1. Saint Augustine, *Confessions*, trans. Henry Chadwick (Oxford: Oxford University Press, 1991), X:xxvii. (p. 201).

2. Alan Loy McGinnis, *The Friendship Factor* (Minneapolis: Augsburg Publishing House, 1979), 27.

3. Martin E. Marty, *Friendship* (Allen, Texas: Argus Communications, 1980), 48.

4. Quoted in Albert McClellen, *Meet Southern Baptists* (Nashville: Broadman Press, 1978), 29–30.

5. J.B. Lightfoot and J.R. Harmer, editors and translators, *The Apostolic Fathers*, second edition (Grand Rapids: Baker Book House, 1992), 541–43; from *The Martyrdom of Polycarp*, 10.

Chapter Ten
1. Edward Gibbon, *The Decline and Fall of the Roman Empire*, available on-line at http://www.worldwideschool.org/library/books/hst/roman/TheDeclineandFallofTheRomanEmpire-1/chap4.html.

2. See http://www.readbookonline.net/readOnLine/3440/.

Conclusion
1. St. Irenaeus, *Against All Heresies*, 4:20:7; English at http://www.gnosis.org/library/advh4.htm. The rest of the sentence is "*vita autem hominis visio Dei*," and the life of a human being is the vision of God.